D1001838

PIPE AND POUCH

PIPE AND POUCH

The SMOKER'S OWN BOOK of POETRY

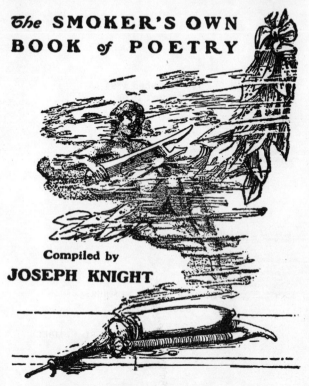

Compiled by

JOSEPH KNIGHT

Granger Index Reprint Series

BOOKS FOR LIBRARIES PRESS

FREEPORT, NEW YORK

First Published 1894
Reprinted 1970

821.008
K69p

STANDARD BOOK NUMBER:
8369-6112-9

LIBRARY OF CONGRESS CATALOG CARD NUMBER:
74-108584

MANUFACTURED
BY
HALLMARK LITHOGRAPHERS, INC.
IN THE U.S.A.

Dedicated

TO MY FRIEND AND FELLOW-SMOKER,

WALTER MONTGOMERY JACKSON.

PREFACE.

THIS is an age of anthologies. Collections of poetry covering a wide range of subjects have appeared of late, and seem to have met with favor and approval. Not to the busy man only, but to the student of literature such compilations are of value. It is sometimes objected that they tend to discourage wide reading and original research; but the overwhelming flood of books would seem to make them a necessity. Unless one has the rare gift of being able to sprint through a book, as Andrew Lang says Mr. Gladstone does, it is surely well to make use of the labors of the industrious compiler. Such collections are often the result of wide reading and patient labor. Frequently the larger part is made up of single poems, the happy and perhaps only inspiration of the writer, gleaned from the poet's corner of the newspaper or the pages of a magazine. This is specially true of the present compilation, the first on the subject aiming at

anything like completeness. Brief collections of
prose and poetry combined have already been
published ; but so much of value has been omitted
that there seemed to be room for a better book.
A vast amount has been written in praise of
tobacco, much of it commonplace or lacking in
poetic quality. While some of the verse here
gathered is an obvious echo, or passes into un-
mistakable parody, it has been the aim of the
compiler to maintain, as far as possible, a high
standard and include only the best. From the
days of Raleigh to the present time, literature
abounds in allusions to tobacco. The Elizabethan
writers constantly refer to it, often in praise though
sometimes in condemnation. The incoming of
the "Indian weed" created a great furore, and
scarcely any other of the New World discoveries
was talked about so much. Ben Jonson, Marlowe,
Fletcher, Spenser, Dekker, and many other of the
poets and dramatists of the time, make frequent
reference to it ; and no doubt at the Mermaid
tavern, pipes and tobacco found a place beside
the sack and ale. Singular to say, Shakespeare
makes no reference to it ; and only once in his
essay "Of Plantations," as far as the compiler has
been able to discover, does Bacon speak of it.
Shakespeare's silence has been explained on the

theory that he could not introduce any reference to the newly discovered plant without anachronism; but he did not often let a little thing of this kind stand in his way. It has been suggested, on the other hand, that he avoided all reference to it out of deference to King James I., who wrote the famous "Counterblast." Whichever theory is correct, the fact remains, and it may be an interesting contribution to the Bacon-Shakespeare controversy. Queen Elizabeth never showed any hostility to tobacco; but her successors, James I. and the two Charleses, and Cromwell were its bitter opponents. Notwithstanding its enemies, who just as fiercely opposed the introduction of tea and coffee, its use spread over Europe and the world, and prince and peasant alike yielded to its mild but irresistible sway. Poets and philosophers drew solace and inspiration from the pipe. Milton, Addison, Fielding, Hobbes, and Newton were all smokers. It is said Newton was smoking under a tree in his garden when the historic apple fell. Scott, Campbell, Byron, Hood, and Lamb all smoked, and Carlyle and Tennyson were rarely without a pipe in their mouths. The great novelists, Thackeray, Dickens, and Bulwer were famous smokers; and so were the great soldiers, Napoleon, Blücher, and Grant. While nearly all the poems here gathered together were written, and perhaps could only have been written, by smokers, several among the best are the work of authors who never use the weed, — one by a man, two or three by women. Among the more recent writers there has been no more devoted smoker than Mr. Lowell, as his recently published letters testify. Three of the most delightful poems in praise of smoking are his, and with Mr. Aldrich's charming "Latakia" are the gems of the collection. The compiler desires to express his grateful acknowledgments to friends who have permitted him to use their work and have otherwise aided him from time to time; and to the many unknown authors whose poems are here gathered, and whom it was quite impossible to reach; and to Messrs. Houghton, Mifflin, & Company, Harper & Brothers, The Bowen-Merrill Company, and the publishers of "Outlook," for their gracious permission to include copyrighted poems.

J. K.

BOSTON, July, 1894.

CONTENTS.

PIPE AND POUCH

PIPE AND POUCH.

WITH PIPE AND BOOK.

WITH Pipe and Book at close of day,
Oh, what is sweeter, mortal, say?
It matters not what book on knee,
Old Izaak or the Odyssey,
It matters not meerschaum or clay.

And though one's eyes will dream astray,
And lips forget to sue or sway,
It is "enough to merely be,"
With Pipe and Book.

What though our modern skies be gray,
As bards aver, I will not pray
For " soothing Death " to succor me,
But ask this much, O Fate, of thee,
A little longer yet to stay
With Pipe and Book.

RICHARD LE GALLIENNE.

A POET'S PIPE.

From the French of Charles Baudelaire.

A POET'S pipe am I,
   And my Abyssinian tint
Is an unmistakable hint
That he lays me not often by.
When his soul is with grief o'erworn
I smoke like the cottage where
They are cooking the evening fare
For the laborer's return.

I enfold and cradle his soul
In the vapors moving and blue
That mount from my fiery mouth;
And there is power in my bowl
To charm his spirit and soothe,
And heal his weariness too.

RICHARD HERNE SHEPHERD.

MY CIGAR.

IN spite of my physician, who is, *entre nous*, a fogy,
   And for every little pleasure has some pathologic
      bogy,
Who will bear with no small vices, and grows dis-
   mally prophetic
If I wander from the weary way of virtue dietetic;

In spite of dire forewarnings that my brains will all
    be scattered,
My memory extinguished, and my nervous system
    shattered,
That my hand will take to trembling, and my heart
    begin to flutter,
My digestion turn a rebel to my very bread and
    butter;

As I puff this mild Havana, and its ashes slowly
    lengthen,
I feel my courage gather and my resolution strengthen:
I will smoke, and I will praise you, my cigar, and I
    will light you
With tobacco-phobic pamphlets by the learnéd prigs
    who fight you!

Let him who has a mistress to her eyebrow write a
    sonnet,
Let the lover of a lily pen a languid ode upon it;
In such sentimental subjects I 'm a Philistine and
    cynic,
And prefer the inspiration drawn from sources
    nicotinic.

So I sing of you, dear product of (I trust you are)
    Havana,
And if there 's any question as to how my verses
    scan, a
Reason is my shyness in the Muses' aid invoking,
As, like other ancient maidens, they perchance object
    to smoking.

I have learnt with you the wisdom of contemplative
   quiescence,
While the world is in a ferment of unmeaning effer-
   vescence,
That its jar and rush and riot bring no good one-half
   so sterling
As your fleecy clouds of fragrance that are now about
   me curling.

So, let stocks go up or downward, and let politicians
   wrangle,
Let the parsons and philosophers grope in a wordy
   tangle,
Let those who want them scramble for their dignities
   or dollars,
Be millionnaires or magnates, or senators or scholars.

I will puff my mild Havana, and I quietly will query,
Whether, when the strife is over, and the combatants
   are weary,
Their gains will be more brilliant than its faint expir-
   ing flashes,
Or more solid than this panful of its dead and sober
   ashes.

                                        ARTHUR W. GUNDRY.

TO C. F. BRADFORD.

On the Gift of a Meerschaum Pipe.

THE pipe came safe, and welcome, too,
   As anything must be from you;
A meerschaum pure, 't would float as light
As she the girls called Amphitrite.
Mixture divine of foam and clay,
From both it stole the best away:
Its foam is such as crowns the glow
Of beakers brimmed by Veuve Clicquot;
Its clay is but congested lymph
Jove chose to make some choicer nymph;
And here combined, — why, this must be
The birth of some enchanted sea,
Shaped to immortal form, the type
And very Venus of a pipe.

When high I heap it with the weed
From Lethe wharf, whose potent seed
Nicotia, big from Bacchus, bore
And cast upon Virginia's shore,
I 'll think, — So fill the fairer bowl
And wise alembic of thy soul,
With herbs far-sought that shall distil,
Not fumes to slacken thought and will,
But bracing essences that nerve
To wait, to dare, to strive, to serve.

When curls the smoke in eddies soft,
And hangs a shifting dream aloft,
That gives and takes, though chance-designed,
The impress of the dreamer's mind,
I 'll think, — So let the vapors bred
By passion, in the heart or head,
Pass off and upward into space,
Waving farewells of tenderest grace,
Remembered in some happier time,
To blend their beauty with my rhyme.

While slowly o'er its candid bowl
The color deepens (as the soul
That burns in mortals leaves its trace
Of bale or beauty on the face),
I 'll think, — So let the essence rare
Of years consuming make me fair;
So, 'gainst the ills of life profuse,
Steep me in some narcotic juice;
And if my soul must part with all
That whiteness which we greenness call,
Smooth back, O Fortune, half thy frown,
And make me beautifully brown!

Dream-forger, I refill thy cup
With reverie's wasteful pittance up,
And while the fire burns slow away,
Hiding itself in ashes gray,
I 'll think, — As inward Youth retreats,
Compelled to spare his wasting heats,

When Life's Ash-Wednesday comes about,
And my head's gray with fires burnt out,
While stays one spark to light the eye,
With the last flash of memory,
'T will leap to welcome C. F. B.,
Who sent my favorite pipe to me.

JAMES RUSSELL LOWELL.

MY PIPE.

WHEN love grows cool, thy fire still warms me;
    When friends are fled, thy presence charms me,
If thou art full, though purse be bare,
I smoke, and cast away all care!

German Smoking Song.

THE FARMER'S PIPE.

MAKE a picture, dreamy smoke,
    In my still and cosey room;
From the fading past evoke
    Forms that breathe of summer's bloom.

Bashful Will and rosy Nell! —
    Ah, I watch them now at play
By the mossy wayside well
    As I did twelve years to-day.

We were younger then, my pipe:
  You are dingy now and worn;
And my fruit is more than ripe,
  And my fields are brown and shorn.

Nell has merry eyes of blue,
  And is timid, pure, and mild;
Will is fair and brave and true,
  And a neighboring farmer's child.

Little maid is busy, too,
  Making rare, fictitious pies,
Just as any wife would do,
  Looking, meanwhile, wondrous wise.

Drawing water from the well,
  Delving sand upon the hill,
Going here and there for Nell, —
  That 's her helpmate, willing Will.

Yonder, in the waning light,
  Hand in hand the truants come,
Nell so fearful lest the night
  Should fall around her far from home.

Fading, fading, skyward flies
  This joy-picture you have limned;
Pipe of mine, the quiet skies
  Of my life you leave undimmed.

Nell and Will are lovers now;
　There they stray in dying light.
That's a kiss!　Ah, well, somehow
　Nell's no more afraid at night!

GEORGE COOPER.

SONG OF THE SMOKE-WREATHS.

Sung to the Smokers.

NOT like clouds that cap the mountains,
　Not like mists that mask the sea,
Not like vapors round the fountains, —
　Soft and clear and warm are we.

Hear the tempest, how its minions
　Tear the clouds and heap the snows!
No storm-rage is in our pinions;
　Who knows us, 't is peace he knows.

Soaring from the burning censers,
　Stealing forth through all the air,
Hovering as the mild dispensers
　Over you of blisses rare,

Softly float we, softly blend we,
　Tinted from the deep blue sky,
Scented from the myrrh-lands, bend we
　Downward to you ere we die.

Ease we bring, and airy fancies,
    Sober thoughts with visions gay,
Peace profound with daring glances
    Through the clouds to endless day.

Not like clouds that cap the mountains,
    Not like mists that mask the sea,
Not like vapors round the fountains, —
    Soft and clear and warm are we.

                L. T. A., in *London Society*.

SMOKE AND CHESS.

WE were sitting at chess as the sun went down;
        And he, from his meerschaum's glossy brown,
With a ring of smoke made his king a crown.

The cherry stem, with its amber tip,
Thoughtfully rested on his lip,
As the goblet's rim from which heroes sip.

And, looking out through the early green,
He called on his patron saint, I ween, —
That misty maiden, Saint Nicotine, —

While ever rested that crown so fair,
Poised in the warm and pulseless air,
On the carven chessman's ivory hair.

Dreamily wandered the game along,
Quietly moving at even-song,
While the striving kings stood firm and **strong,**

Until that one which of late was crowned
Flinched from a knight's determined bound,
And in sullen majesty left the ground,

Reeling back; and it came to pass
That, waiting to mutter no funeral mass,
A bishop had dealt him the *coup de grace.*

And so, as we sat, we reasoned still
Of fate and of fortune, of human will,
And what are the purposes men fulfil.

For we see at last, when the truth arrives,
The moves on the chess-board of our lives, —
That fields may be lost, though the king survives.

Not always he whom the world reveres
Merits its honor or wins its cheers,
Standing the best at the end of the years.

Not always he who has lost the fight
Rises again with the coming light,
Battles anew for his ancient right.

SAMUEL W. DUFFIELD.

INSCRIPTION FOR A TOBACCO JAR.

KEEP me at hand; and as my fumes arise,
   You'll find *a jar* the gates of Paradise.
                              Copes Tobacco Plant.

MOTTO FOR A TOBACCO JAR.

COME! don't refuse sweet Nicotina's aid,
   But woo the goddess through a yard of clay;
And soon you'll own she is the fairest maid
   To stifle pain, and drive old Care away.
Nor deem it waste ; what though to ash she burns,
If for your outlay you get good returns!

THE LAST PIPE.

WHEN head is sick and brain doth swim,
   And heavy hangs each unstrung limb,
'T is sweet through smoke-puffs, wreathing slow,
To watch the firelight flash or glow.
As each soft cloud floats up on high,
Some worry takes its wings to fly;
And Fancy dances with the flame,
Who lay so labor-crammed and lame ;
While the spent Will, the slack Desire,
Re-kindle at the dying fire,
And burn to meet the morrow's sun
With all its day's work to be done.

The tedious tangle of the Law,
Your work ne'er done without some flaw;
Those ghastly streets that drive one mad,
With children joyless, elders sad,
Young men unmanly, girls going by
Bold-voiced, with eyes unmaidenly;
Christ dead two thousand years agone,
And kingdom come still all unwon;
Your own slack self that will not rise
Whole-hearted for the great emprise, —
Well, all these dark thoughts of the day
As thin smoke's shadow drift away.

And all those magic mists unclose,
And a girl's face amid them grows, —
The very look she 's wont to wear,
The wild rose blossoms in her hair,
The wondrous depths of her pure eyes,
The maiden soul that 'neath them lies,
That fears to meet, yet will not fly,
Your stranger spirit drawing nigh.
What if our times seem sliding down?
She lives, creation's flower and crown.
What if your way seems dull and long?
Each tiny triumph over wrong,
Each effort up through sloth and fear,
And she and you are brought more near.
So rapping out these ashes light, —
" My pipe, you've served me well to-night."

London Spectator.

ODE TO MY PIPE.

O BLESSED pipe,
     That now I clutch within my gripe,
What joy is in thy smooth, round bowl,
          As black as coal!

So sweetly wed
To thy blanched, gradual thread,
Like Desdemona to the Moor,
          Thou pleasure's core.

What woman's lip
Could ever give, like thy red tip,
Such unremitting store of bliss,
          Or such a kiss?

Oh, let me toy,
Ixion-like, with cloudy joy;
Thy stem with a most gentle slant
          I eye askant!

Unseen, unheard,
Thy dreamy nectar is transferred,
The while serenity astride
          Thy neck doth ride.

A burly cloud
Doth now thy outward beauties shroud;
And now a film doth upward creep,
          Cuddling the cheek.

And now a ring,
A mimic silver quoit, takes wing;
Another and another mount on high,
    Then spread and die.

They say in story
That good men have a crown of glory;
O beautiful and good, behold
    The crowns unfold!

How did they live?
What pleasure could the Old World give
That ancient miserable lot
    When thou wert not?

Oh, woe betide!
My oldest, dearest friend hath died, —
Died in my hand quite unaware,
    Oh, Baccy rare!
              ANDREW WYNTER.

A PIPE OF TOBACCO.

LET the toper regale in his tankard of ale,
  Or with alcohol moisten his thrapple,
Only give me, I pray, a good pipe of soft clay,
  Nicely tapered and thin in the stapple;
And I shall puff, puff, let who will say, "Enough!"
  No luxury else I 'm in lack o',
No malice I hoard 'gainst queen, prince, duke, or lord,
  While I pull at my pipe of tobacco.

When I feel the hot strife of the battle of life,
  And the prospect is aught but encitin',
Mayhap some real ill, like a protested bill,
  Dims the sunshine that tinged the horizon:
Only let me puff, puff, — be they ever so rough,
  All the sorrows of life I lose track o',
The mists disappear, and the vista is clear,
  With a soothing mild pipe of tobacco.

And when joy after pain, like the sun after rain,
  Stills the waters, long turbid and troubled,
That life's current may flow with a ruddier glow,
  And the sense of enjoyment be doubled, —
Oh! let me puff, puff, till I feel *quantum suff.*,
  Such luxury still I 'm in lack o';
Be joy ever so sweet, it would be incomplete,
  Without a good pipe of tobacco.

Should my recreant muse — sometimes apt to refuse
  The guidance of bit and of bridle —
Still blankly demur, spite of whip and spur,
  Unimpassioned, inconstant, or idle;
Only let me puff, puff, till the brain cries, "Enough!'
  Such excitement is all I 'm in lack o',
And the poetic vein soon to fancy gives rein,
  Inspired by a pipe of tobacco.

And when, with one accord, round the jovial board,
  In friendship our bosoms are glowing,
While with toast and with song we the evening prolong,
  And with nectar the goblets are flowing;

Still let us puff, puff, — be life smooth, be it rough,
  Such enjoyment we 're ever in lack o';
The more peace and good-will will abound as we fill
  A jolly good pipe of tobacco.

JOHN USHER.

EPITAPH

*On a Young Lady who Desired that Tobacco Might be Planted
Over her Grave.*

LET no cold marble o'er my body rise —
    But only earth above, and sunny skies.
Thus would I lowly lie in peaceful rest,
Nursing the Herb Divine from out my breast.
Green let it grow above this clay of mine,
Deriving strength from strength that I resign.
So in the days to come, when I 'm beyond
This fickle life, will come my lovers fond,
And gazing on the plant, their grief restrain
In whispering, " Lo! dear Anna blooms again!"

THE SMOKER'S REVERIE.

(*October.*)

I 'M sitting at dusk 'neath the old beechen tree,
    With its leaves by the autumn made ripe;
While they cling to the stems like old age unto life,
I dream of the days when I 'll rest from this strife,
    And in peace smoke my brierwood pipe.

O my brierwood pipe!—of bright fancy the twin,
    What a medley of forms you create;
Every puff of white smoke seems a vision as fair
As the poet's bright dream, and like dreams fades in
        air,
    While the dreamer dreams on of his fate.

The fleecy white clouds that now float in the sky,
    Form the visions I love most to see;
Fairy shapes that I saw in my boyhood's first dreams
Seem to beckon me on, while beyond them there
        gleams
    A bright future, in waiting for me.

O my brierwood pipe!   I ne'er loved thee as now,
    As that fair form and face steal above;
See, she beckons me on to where roses are spread,
And she points to my fancy the bright land ahead,
    Where the winds whisper nothing but love.

Oh, answer, my pipe, shall my dream be as fair
    When it changes to dreams of the past?
When autumn's chill winds make this leaf look as sere
As the leaves on the beech-tree that shelters me here,
    Will the tree's *heart* be chilled by the blast?

While musing, around me has gathered a heap
    Of the leaflets, all dying and dead;
And I see in my reverie plainly revealed
The slope of life's hill, in my boyhood concealed
    By the forms that fair fancy had bred.

While I sit on the banks of the beautiful stream,
 Picking roses that bloom by its side,
I know that the shallop will certainly come,
When the roses are withered, to carry me home,
 And that life will go out with the tide.

O my brierwood pipe! may the heart be as light
 When memory supplanteth the dream;
When the sun has gone down may the sunbeam
  remain,
And life's roses, though dead, all their fragrance retain,
 Till they catch at Eternity's gleam.

ANON.

A BRIEF PUFF OF SMOKE.

GREAT Doctor Parr, the learned Whig,
 Ne'er deemed the smoke-cloud *infra dig.*,
In which you could not see his wig,
  Involved in clouds of smoke.

Quaint Lamb his wit would oft enshroud
In smoke-igniting laughter loud,
Like summer thunder in the cloud, —
  The lightning in the smoke.

Dean Swift "died at the top;" his head
Had drifting clouds when wit had fled:
Dull care lurked in his brain, instead
  Of blowing out in smoke.

And Cowper mild — no smoker he,
Bard of the sofa and bohea —
Complained his " dear friend Bull " not free
    From lowering Stygian smoke.

Clouds in his non-inebriate nob
Were doomed the tea tables to rob,
Inflicting many a painful throb
    On one who could not smoke !

Smoke on ! it is the steam of life,
The smoother of the waves of strife ;
Where chimneys smoke, or scolds the wife,
    The counteraction — smoke.

We ride and work and weave by steam,
Till ages past seem like a dream
In a new world whose dawning beam
    Is redolent of smoke.

We travel like a comet wild
On which some distant sun had smiled,
And from his orbit thus beguiled
    With a long tail of smoke.

The clouds arise from smoking seas,
And give, with each conveying breeze,
Life to the " weed," and herbs, and trees,
    Which turn again to smoke.

All nations smoke! Havana's pother
Smokes friendly with its Broseley brother:
The world's one end puffs to the other,
     In amicable smoke.

When plague and pestilence go forth,
And to diseases dire give birth,
Which walk in darkness through the earth,
     I clothe myself in smoke.

I smoke through desolating years,
Tabooed from fever, void of fears,
And when some dreaded pest appears,
     I call in Doctor Smoke.

Go, reader! perfume ladies' hair
And scent the ringlets of the fair
With eau Cologne and odors rare
     Aloof from healthy smoke.

Go babble at the ball and rout,
And smirk with high-born dames who doubt.
Thy flames are quenched, thy fires are out,
     And sinking into smoke.

"Better," said Johnson, great in name,
"It were, when poets droop in fame,
To see smoke brighten into flame,
     Than flames sink into smoke."
           SELIM: *Eclectic Magazine.*

A SYMPHONY IN SMOKE.

A PRETTY, piquant, pouting pet,
    Who likes to muse and take her ease,
She loves to smoke a cigarette;

To dream in silken hammockette,
And sing and swing beneath the trees,
A pretty, piquant, pouting pet.

Her Christian name is Violet;
Her eyes are blue as summer skies;
She loves to smoke a cigarette.

As calm as babe in bassinette,
She swingeth in the summer breeze,
A pretty, piquant, pouting pet.

She ponders o'er a novelette;
Her parasol is Japanese;
She loves to smoke a cigarette.

She loves a fume without a fret;
Her frills are white, her frock *cérise,* —
A pretty, pouting, piquant pet.

She almost goes to sleep, and yet,
Half-lulled by booming honey-bees,
She loves to smoke a cigarette.

A winsome, clever, cool coquette,
Who flouts all Grundian decrees, —
A pretty, pouting, piquant pet,
That loves to smoke a cigarette.

Harper's Bazar.

IT MAY BE WEEDS.

IT may be weeds
   I 've gathered too;
But even weeds may be
   As fragrant as
   The fairest flower
With some sweet memory.

ANON.

SEASONABLE SWEETS.

" Don't be flowery, Jacob." — CHARLES DICKENS.

WHEN the year is young, what sweets are flung
   By the violets, hiding, dim,
And the lilac that sways her censers high,
   Whilst the skylark chants a hymn !
How sweet is the scent of the daffodil bloom,
   When blithe spring decks each spray,
And the flowering thorn sheds rare perfume
   Through the beautiful month of May !
What a dainty pet is the mignonette,
   Whose sweets wide scattered are !
But sweeter to me than all these yet
   Is the scent of a prime cigar !

Delicious airs waft the fields of June,
  When the beans are all in flower;
The woodruff is fragrant in the hedge,
  And the woodbine in the bower.
Sweet eglantine doth her garlands twine
  For the blithe hours as they run,
And balmily sighs the meadow-sweet,
  That is all in love with the sun,
Whilst new-mown hay o'er the hedgerows gay
  Flings odorous airs afar;
Yet sweeter than these on the passing breeze
  Is the scent of a prime cigar.

When all the beauties of Flora's court
  Smile on the gay parterre,
What glorious color, what exquisite form,
  And dainty scents are there !
They bask in the beam, and bend by the stream,
  Like beautiful nymphs at play,
Holding dew-pearls up in each nectar cup
  To the glorious God of Day.
Oh, their lives are sweet, but all too brief,
  And death doth their sweetness mar;
But fragrance fine is forever thine,
  My well-beloved cigar !

                                        C.

GEORDIE TO HIS TOBACCO-PIPE.

GOOD pipe, old friend, old black and colored friend,
   Whom I have smoked these fourteen years and
     more,
My best companion, faithful to the end,
Faithful to death through all thy fiery core,

How shall I sing thy praises, or proclaim
The generous virtues which I 've found in thee?
I know thou carest not a whit for fame,
And hast no thought but how to comfort me,

And serve my needs, and humor every mood;
But love and friendship do my heart constrain
To give thee all I can for much of good
Which thou hast rendered me in joy and pain.

Say, then, old honest meerschaum! shall I weave
Thy history together with my own?
Of late I never see thee but I grieve
For him whose gift thou wert — forever gone!

Gone to his grave amidst the vines of France,
He, all so good, so beautiful, and wise;
And this dear giver doth thyself enhance,
And makes thee doubly precious in mine eyes.

For he was one of Nature's rarest men, —
Poet and preacher, lover of his kind,
True-hearted man of God, whose like again
In this world's journey I may never find.

I know not if the shadow of his soul,
Or the divine effulgence of his heart,
Has through thy veins in mystic silence stole;
But thou to me dost seem of him a part.

His hands have touched thee, and his lips have
        drawn,
As mine, full many an inspiring cloud
From thy great burning heart, at night and morn;
And thou art here, whilst he lies in his shroud!

And here am I, his friend and thine, old pipe!
And he has often sat my chair beside,
As he was wont to sit in living type,
Of many companies the flower and pride, —

Sat by my side, and talked to me the while,
Invisible to every eye save mine,
And smiled upon me as he used to smile
When we three sat o'er our good cups of wine.

Ah, happy days, when the old Chapel House,
Of the old Forest Chapel, rang with mirth.
And the great joy of our divine carouse,
As we hobnobbed it by the blazing hearth!

We never more, old pipe, shall see those days,
Whose memories lie like pictures in my mind;
But thou and I will go the self-same ways,
E'en though we leave all other friends behind.

And for thy sake, and for my own, and his,
We will be one, as we have ever been,
Thou dear old friend, with thy most honest phiz,
And no new faces come our loves between.

II.

Thou hast thy separate virtues, honest pipe!
Apart from all the memory of friends;
For thou art mellow, old, and black, and ripe;
And the good weed that in its smoke ascends

From thy rare bowl doth scent the liberal air
With incense richer than the woods of Ind.
E'en to the barren palate of despair
(Inhaled through cedar tubes from glorious Scinde!)

It hath a charm would quicken into life,
And make the heart gush out in streams of love,
And the earth, dead before, with beauty rife,
And full of flowers as heaven of stars above.

It is thy virtue and peculiar gift,
Thou sooty wizard of the potent weed;
No other pipe can thus the soul uplift,
Or such rare fancies and high musings breed.

I 've tried full many of thy kith and kind,
Dug from thy native Asiatic clay,
Fashioned by cunning hand and curious mind
Into all shapes and features, grave and gay, —

Black niggers' heads with their white-livered eyes
Glaring in fiery horror through the smoke,
And monstrous dragons stained with bloody dyes,
And comelier forms; but all save thee I broke.

For though, like thee, each pipe was black and old,
They were not wiser for their many years,
Nor knew thy sorcery though set in gold,
Nor had thy tropic taste, — these proud compeers!

Like great John Paul, who would have loved thee well,
Thou art the "only one" of all thy race;
Nor shall another comrade near thee dwell,
Old King of pipes! my study's pride and grace!

III.

Thus have I made "assurance doubly sure,"
And sealed it twice, that thou shalt reign alone!
And as the dainty bee doth search for pure,
Sweet honey till his laden thighs do groan

With their sweet burden, tasting nothing foul,
So thou of best tobacco shalt be filled;
And when the starry midnight wakes the owl,
And the lorn nightingale her song has trilled,

I, with my lamp and books, as is my wont,
Will give thee of the choicest of all climes, —
Black Cavendish, full-flavored, full of juice,
Pale Turkish, famed through all the Osman times,

Dark Latakia, Syrian, Persia's pride,
And sweet Virginian, sweeter than them all!
Oh, rich bouquet of plants! fit for a bride
Who, blushing, waits the happy bridegroom's call!

And these shall be thy food, thy dainty food,
And we together will their luxury share,
Voluptuous tumults stealing through the blood,
Voluptuous visions filling all the air!

I will not thee profane with impious shag,
Nor poison thee with nigger-head and twist,
Nor with Kentucky, though the planters brag
That it hath virtues all the rest have missed.

These are for porters, loafers, and the scum,
Who have no sense for the diviner weeds,
Who drink their muddy beer and muddier rum,
Insatiate, like dogs in all their greeds.

But not for thee nor me these things obscene;
We have a higher pleasure, purer taste.
My draughts have been with thee of hippocrene,
And our delights intelligent and chaste.

IV.

Intelligent and chaste since we have held
Commune together on the world's highway;
No Falstaff failings have my mind impelled
To do misdeeds of sack by night or day;

But we have ever erred on virtue's side —
At least we should have done — but woe is me!
I fear in this my statement I have lied,
For ghosts, like moonlight shadows on the sea,

Crowd thick around me from the shadowy past, —
Ghosts of old memories reeling drunk with wine!
And boon companions, Lysius-like, and vast
In their proportions as the god divine.

I do confess my sins, and here implore
The aid of " Rare Old Ben " and other ghosts
That I may sin again, but rarely more,
Responsive only unto royal toasts.

For, save these sins, I am a saintly man,
And live like other saints on prayer and praise,
My long face longer, if life be a span,
Than any two lives in these saintly days.

So let me smoke and drink and do good deeds,
And boast the doing like a Pharisee ;
Am I not holy if I love the creeds,
Even though my drinking sins choke up the sea?

GEORGE S. PHILLIPS (JANUARY SEARLE):
The Gypsies of the Dane's Dike.

INVOCATION TO TOBACCO.

WEED of the strange flower, weed of the earth,
  Killer of dulness, parent of mirth,
Come in the sad hour, come in the gay,
Appear in the night, or in the day, —
Still thou art welcome as June's blooming rose,
Joy of the palate, delight of the nose.

Weed of the green field, weed of the wild,
Fostered in freedom, America's child,
Come in Virginia, come in Havana,
Friend of the universe, sweeter than manna, —
Still thou art welcome, rich, fragrant, and ripe,
Pride of the tube-case, delight of the pipe.

Weed of the savage, weed of each pole,
Comforting, soothing, philosophy's soul,
Come in the snuff-box, come in cigar,
In Strasburgh and King's, come from afar, —
Still thou art welcome, the purest, the best,
Joy of earth's millions, forever carest.

HENRY JAMES MELLEN.

VIRGINIA TOBACCO.

TWO maiden dames of sixty-two
  Together long had dwelt;
Neither, alas! of love so true
  The bitter pang had felt.

But age comes on, they say, apace,
    To warn us of our death,
And wrinkles mar the fairest face, —
    At last it stops our breath.

One of these dames tormented sore
    With that curst pang, toothache,
Was at a loss for such a bore
    What remedy to take.

"I've heard," thought she, "this ill to cure,
    A pipe is good, they say.
Well then, tobacco I'll endure,
    And smoke the pain away."

The pipe was lit, the tooth soon well,
    And she retired to rest,
When then the other ancient belle
    Her spinster maid addressed, —

"Let me request a favor, pray" —
    "I'll do it if I can" —
"Oh! well, then, love, smoke every day,
    You smell so like a man!"

Attributed to JOHN STANLEY GREGSON.

AN ODE OF THANKS FOR CERTAIN CIGARS.

To Charles Eliot Norton.

LUCK, my dear Norton, still makes shifts,
    To mix a mortal with her gifts,
Which he may find who duly sifts.

Sweets to the sweet, — behold the clue!
Why not, then, new things to the gnu,
And trews to Highland clansmen true?

'T was thus your kindly thought decreed
These weeds to one who is indeed,
And feels himself, a very weed, —

A weed from which, when bruised and shent,
Though some faint perfume may be rent,
Yet oftener much without a cent.

But imp, O Muse, a stronger wing
Mount, leaving self below, and sing
What thoughts these Cuban exiles bring!

He that knows aught of mythic lore
Knows how god Bacchus wandered o'er
The earth, and what strange names he bore.

The Bishop of Avranches supposes
That all these large and varying doses
Of fable mean naught else than Moses;

But waiving doubts, we surely know
He taught mankind to plough and sow,
And from the Tigris to the Po

Planted the vine; but of his visit
To this our hemisphere, why is it
We have no statement more explicit?

He gave to us a leaf divine
More grateful to the serious Nine
Than fierce inspirings of the vine.

And that *he* loved it more, this proved, —
He gave his name to what he loved,
Distorted now, but not removed.

Tobacco, sacred herb, though lowly,
Baffles old Time, the tyrant, wholly,
And makes him turn his hour-glass slowly;

Nay, makes as 't were of every glass six,
Whereby we beat the heathen classics
With their weak Chians and their Massics.

These gave his glass a quicker twist,
And flew the hours like driving mist,
While Horace drank and Lesbia kissed.

How are we gainers when all 's done,
If Life's swift clepsydra have run
With wine for water?   'T is all one.

But this rare plant delays the stream
(At least if things are what they seem)
Through long eternities of dream.

What notes the antique Muse had known
Had she, instead of oat-straws, blown
Our wiser pipes of clay or stone!

Rash song, forbear! Thou canst not hope,
Untutored as thou art, to cope
With themes of such an epic scope.

Enough if thou give thanks to him
Who sent these leaves (forgive the whim)
Plucked from the dream-tree's sunniest limb.

My gratitude feels no eclipse,
For I, whate'er my other slips,
Shall have his kindness on my lips.

The prayers of Christian, Turk, and Jew
Have one sound up there in the blue,
And one smell all their incense, too.

Perhaps that smoke with incense ranks
Which curls from 'mid life's jars and clanks,
Graceful with happiness and thanks.

I pledge him, therefore, in a puff, —
A rather frailish kind of stuff,
But still professional enough.

Hock-cups breed hiccups ; let us feel
The god along our senses steel
More nobly and without his reel.

Each temperately 'baccy *plenus,*
May no grim fate of doubtful genus
E'er blow the smallest cloud between us.

And as his gift I shall devote
To fire, and o'er their ashes gloat, —
Let him do likewise with this note.

JAMES RUSSELL LOWELL.

[From "The Letters of James Russell Lowell." Copyright, 1893, by Harper & Brothers.]

AN ENCOMIUM ON TOBACCO.

THRICE happy isles that stole the world's delight,
   And thus produce so rich a Margarite!
It is the fountain whence all pleasure springs,
A potion for imperial and mighty kings.

He that is master of so rich a store
May laugh at Crœsus and esteem him poor ;
And with his smoky sceptre in his fist,
Securely flout the toiling alchemist,
Who daily labors with a vain expense
In distillations of the quintessence,
Not knowing that this golden herb alone
Is the philosopher's admired stone.

It is a favor which the gods doth please,
If they do feed on smoke, as Lucian says.
Therefore the cause that the bright sun doth rest
At the low point of the declining west —
When his oft-wearied horses breathless pant —
Is to refresh himself with this sweet plant,
Which wanton Thetis from the west doth bring,
To joy her love after his toilsome ring:
For 't is a cordial for an inward smart,
As is dictamnum to the wounded hart.
It is the sponge that wipes out all our woe;
'T is like the thorn that doth on Pelion grow,
With which whoe'er his frosty limbs anoints,
Shall feel no cold in fat or flesh or joints.
'T is like the river, which whoe'er doth taste
Forgets his present griefs and sorrows past.
Music, which makes grim thoughts retire,
And for a while cease their tormenting fire, —
Music, which forces beasts to stand and gaze,
And fills their senseless spirits with amaze, —
Compared to this is like delicious strings,
Which sound but harshly while Apollo sings.
The train with this infumed, all quarrel ends,
And fiercest foemen turn to faithful friends;
The man that shall this smoky magic prove,
Will need no philtres to obtain his love.

Yet the sweet simple, by misordered use,
Death or some dangerous sickness may produce.
Should we not for our sustentation eat
Because a surfeit comes from too much meat?

So our fair plant — that doth as needful stand
As heaven, or fire, or air, or sea, or land;
As moon, or stars that rule the gloomy night,
Or sacred friendship, or the sunny light —
Her treasured virtue in herself enrolls,
And leaves the evil to vainglorious souls.
And yet, who dies with this celestial breath
Shall live immortal in a joyful death.
All goods, all pleasures it in one can link —
'T is physic, clothing, music, meat, and drink.

Gods would have revell'd at their feasts of mirth
With this pure distillation of the earth;
The marrow of the world, star of the West,
The pearl whereby this lower orb is blest;
The joy of mortals, umpire of all strife,
Delight of nature, mithridate of life;
The daintiest dish of a delicious feast,
By taking which man differs from a beast.

ANONYMOUS : *Time, James I.*

ON A TOBACCO JAR.

THREE hundred years ago or soe,
　　One worthy knight and gentlemanne
Did bring me here, to charm and chere,
　　To physical and mental manne.
God bless his soule who filled ye bowle,
　　And may our blessings find him;
That he not miss some share of blisse
　　Who left soe much behind him.

BERNARD BARKER.

TO THE TOBACCO PIPE.

DEAR piece of fascinating clay!
   'T is thine to smooth life's rugged **way,**
To give a happiness unknown
To those — who let a pipe alone;
Thy tube can best the vapors chase,
By raising — others in their place;
Can give the face staid Wisdom's air,
And teach the lips — to ope with care;
'T is hence thou art the truest friend
(Where least is said there 's least to mend),
And he who ventures many a joke
Had better oft be still and smoke.

Whatever giddy foplings think,
Thou giv'st the highest zest to drink.
When fragrant clouds thy fumes exhale,
And hover round the nut-brown ale,
Who thinks of claret or champagne?
E'en burgundy were pour'd in vain.

'T is not in city smoke alone,
Midst fogs and glooms thy charms are **known.**
With thee, at morn, the rustic swain
Tracks o'er the snow-besprinkled plain,
To seek some neighb'ring copse's side,
And rob the woodlands of their **pride;**

With thee, companion of his toil,
His active spirits ne'er recoil;
Though hard his daily task assign'd,
He bears it with an equal mind.

The fisher 'board some little bark,
When all around is drear and dark,
With shortened pipe beguiles the hour,
Though bleak the wind and cold the show'r,
Nor thinks the morn's approach too slow,
Regardless of what tempests blow.
Midst hills of sand, midst ditches, dikes,
Midst cannons, muskets, halberts, pikes;
With thee, as still, Mynheer can stay,
As Neddy 'twixt two wisps of hay;
Heedless of Britain and of France,
Smokes on — and looks to the main chance.

And sure the solace thou canst give
Must make thy fame unrivalled live,
So long as men can temper clay
(For as thou art, e'en so are they),
The sun mature the Indian weed,
And rolling years fresh sorrows breed.

From *The Meteors*, London.

THE PATRIOTIC SMOKER'S LAMENT.

TELL me, shade of Walter Raleigh,
     Briton of the truest type,
When that too devoted valet
     Quenched your first-recorded pipe,
Were you pondering the opinion,
     As you watched the airy coil,
That the virtue of Virginia
     Might be bred in British soil?

You transplanted the potato,
     'T was a more enduring gift
Than the wisdom of a Plato
     To our poverty and thrift.
That respected root has flourished
     Nobly for a nation's need,
But our brightest dreams are nourished
     Ever on a foreign weed.

From the deepest meditation
     Of the philosophic scribe,
From the poet's inspiration,
     For the cynic's polished gibe,
We invoke narcotic nurses
     In their jargon from afar,
I indite these modest verses
     On a polyglot cigar.

Leaf that lulls a Turkish Aga
  May a scholar's soul renew,
Fancy spring from Larranaga,
  History from honey-dew.
When the teacher and the tyro
  Spirit-manna fondly seek,
'T is the cigarette from Cairo,
  Or a compound from the Greek.

But no British-born aroma
  Is fit incense to the Queen,
Nature gives her best diploma
  To the alien nicotine.
We are doomed to her ill-favor,
  For the plant that 's native grown
Has a patriotic flavor
  Too exclusively our own.

O my country, could your smoker
  Boast your " shag," or even " twist,"
Every man were mediocre
  Save the blest tobacconist!
He will point immortal morals,
  Make all common praises mute,
Who shall win our grateful laurels
  With a national cheroot.

                    The St. James Gazette.

TO AN OLD PIPE.

ONCE your smoothly polished face
　　Nestled lightly in a case;
'T was a jolly cosy place,
　　　　I surmise;

And a zealous subject blew
On your cheeks, until they grew
To the fascinating hue
　　　　Of her eyes.

Near a rusty-hilted sword,
Now upon my mantel-board,
Where my curios are stored,
　　　　You recline.

You were pleasant company when
By the scribbling of her pen
I was sent the ways of men
　　　　To repine.

Tell me truly (you were there
When she ceased that debonair
Correspondence and affair) —
　　　　I suppose

That she laughed and smiled all day;
Or did gentle tear-drops stray
Down her charming *retroussée*
　　　　Little nose?

Where the sunbeams, coyly **still,**
Fall upon the mantel-sill,
You perpetually will
             Silence woo;

And I fear that she herself,
By the little chubby elf,
Will be laid upon the shelf
             Just as you.

DE WITT STERRY.

TITLEPAGE DEDICATION.

" L ET those smoke now who never smoked before,
   And those who always smoked — now smoke
       the more."

ACROSTIC.

T O thee, blest weed, whose sovereign wiles,
O'er cankered care bring radiant smiles,
Best gift of Love to mortals given!
At once the bud and bliss of Heaven!
Crownless are kings uncrowned by thee;
Content the serf in thy sweet liberty,
O charm of life!   O foe to misery!

J. H.

ANOTHER MATCH.

After A. C. Swinburne.

IF love were dhudeen olden
  And I were like the weed,
Oh! we would live together
And love the jolly weather,
And bask in sunshine golden,
  Rare pals of choicest breed;
If love were dhudeen olden,
  And I were like the weed.

If you were oil essential,
  And I were nicotine,
We'd hatch up wicked treason,
And spoil each smoker's reason,
Till he grew penitential,
  And turned a bilious green;
If you were oil essential,
  And I were nicotine.

If you were snuff, my darling,
  And I, your love, the box,
We'd live and sneeze together,
Shut out from all the weather,
And anti-snuffers snarling,
  In neckties orthodox;
If you were snuff, my darling,
  And I, your love, the box.

If you were the aroma,
　　And I were simply smoke,
We 'd skyward fly together,
As light as any feather;
And flying high as Homer,
　　His gray old ghost we 'd choke;
If you were the aroma,
　　And I were simply smoke.

From Cope's Tobacco Plant.

IN WREATHS OF SMOKE.

IN wreaths of smoke, blown waywardwise,
　Faces of olden days uprise,
　　And in his dreamers revery
　They haunt the smoker's brain, and he
Breathes for the past regretful sighs.

　　Mem'ries of maids, with azure eyes,
　　In dewy dells, 'neath June's soft skies,
　　　Faces that more he 'll only see
　　　In wreaths of smoke.

Eheu, eheu! how fast Time flies, —
How youth-time passion droops and dies,
　And all the countless visions flee!
　How worn would all those faces be,
Were they not swathed in soft disguise
　　In wreaths of smoke!

FRANK NEWTON HOLMAN.

ASHES.

WRAPPED in a sadly tattered gown,
  Alone I puff my brier brown,
And watch the ashes settle down
    In lambent flashes;
While thro' the blue, thick, curling haze,
I strive with feeble eyes to gaze,
Upon the half-forgotten days
    That left but ashes.

Again we wander through the lane,
Beneath the elms and out again,
Across the rippling fields of grain,
    Where softly flashes
A slender brook 'mid banks of fern,
At every sigh my pulses burn,
At every thought I slowly turn
    And find but ashes.

What made my fingers tremble so,
As you wrapped skeins of worsted snow,
Around them, now with movements slow
    And now with dashes?
Maybe 'tis smoke that blinds my eyes,
Maybe a tear within them lies;
But as I puff my pipe there flies
    A cloud of ashes.

Perhaps you did not understand,
How lightly flames of love were fanned.
Ah, every thought and wish I 've planned
    With something clashes!
And yet within my lonely den
Over a pipe, away from men,
I love to throw aside my pen
    And stir the ashes.

                        DE WITT STERRY.

CHOOSING A WIFE BY A PIPE OF TOBACCO.

TUBE, I love thee as my life;
    By thee I mean to choose a wife.
Tube, thy *color* let me find,
In her *skin*, and in her *mind*.
Let her have a *shape* as fine;
Let her breath be sweet as thine;
Let her, when her lips I kiss,
Burn like thee, to give me bliss;
Let her, in some *smoke* or other,
All my failings kindly smother.
Often when my thoughts are *low*,
Send them where they ought to go;
When to study I incline,
Let her aid be such as thine;
Such as thine the charming power
In the vacant social hour.

Let her live to give delight,
Ever *warm* and ever *bright;*
Let her deeds, whene'er she dies,
Mount as incense to the skies.

Gentleman's Magazine.

MY THREE LOVES.

WHEN Life was all a summer day,
   And I was under twenty,
Three loves were scattered in my way —
And three at once are plenty.
Three hearts, if offered with a grace,
One thinks not of refusing;
The task in this especial case
Was only that of choosing.
   I knew not which to make my pet, —
   My pipe, cigar, or cigarette.

To cheer my night or glad my day
My pipe was ever willing;
The meerschaum or the lowly clay
Alike repaid the filling.
Grown men delight in blowing clouds,
As boys in blowing bubbles,
Our cares to puff away in crowds
And vanish all our troubles.
   My pipe I nearly made my pet,
   Above cigar or cigarette.

A tiny paper, tightly rolled
About some Latakia,
Contains within its magic fold
A mighty *panacea.*
Some thought of sorrow or of strife
At ev'ry whiff will vanish;
And all the scenery of life
Turn picturesquely Spanish.
        But still I could not quite forget
        Cigar and pipe for cigarette.

To yield an after-dinner puff
O'er *demi-tasse* and brandy,
No cigarettes are strong enough,
No pipes are ever handy.
However fine may be the feed,
It only moves my laughter
Unless a dry delicious weed
Appears a little after.
        A prime cigar I firmly set
        Above a pipe or cigarette.

But after all I try in vain
To fetter my opinion;
Since each upon my giddy brain
Has boasted a dominion.
Comparisons I 'll not provoke,
Lest *all* should be offended.

Let this discussion end in smoke
As many more have ended.
    And each I 'll make a special pet;
    My pipe, cigar, and cigarette.

                  HENRY S. LEIGH.

SMOKE IS THE FOOD OF LOVERS.

WHEN Cupid open'd shop, the trade he chose
    Was just the very one you might suppose.
Love keep a shop? — his trade, oh! quickly name!
A dealer in tobacco — fie, for shame!
No less than true, and set aside all joke,
From oldest time he ever dealt in smoke;
Than smoke, no other thing he sold, or made;
Smoke all the substance of his stock in trade;
His capital all smoke, smoke all his store,
'T was nothing else; but lovers ask no more —
And thousands enter daily at his door!
Hence it was ever, and it e'er will be
The trade most suited to his faculty:
Fed by the vapors of their heart's desire,
No other food his votaries require;
For that they seek — the favor of the fair —
Is unsubstantial as the smoke and air.

        JACOB CATS: *Moral Emblems.*

CLOUDS.

MORTALS say their heart is light
    When the clouds around disperse;
Clouds to gather, thick as night,
Is the smoker's universe.

From the German of Bauernfeld.

IN FAVOR OF TOBACCO.

MUCH victuals serves for gluttony
    To fatten men like swine;
But he 's a frugal man indeed
That with a leaf can dine,
And needs no napkin for his hands,
His fingers' ends to wipe,
But keeps his kitchen in a box,
And roast meat in a pipe.

SAMUEL ROWLANDS:
Knave of Clubs (1611)

MY CIGARETTE.

Words and music by Richard Barnard.

TO my sweet cigarette I am singing
    This joyous and bright bacca-role;
Just now to my lips she was clinging,
    Her spirit was soothing my soul.

With figure so slender and dapper
　I feel the soft touch of it yet,
Adorned in her dainty white wrapper,
　How fair is my own cigarette!
　　　'T were better, perhaps, that we part, love;
　　　'T were better, if never we 'd met.
　　　Alas, you are part of my heart, love,
　　　Destructive but sweet cigarette!

Though matchless, by matches she 's fired,
　And glows both with pleasure and pride;
By her soft, balmy breath I 'm inspired,
　And kiss and caress my new bride.
E'en the clouds of her nature are joyous,
　Though other clouds cause us regret;
From worry and care they decoy us,
　The clouds of a sweet cigarette.
　　　'T were better, etc.

The houris in paradise living
　Dissolve in the first love embrace,
Their life to their love freely giving, —
　And so with my love 't is the case;
For when her life's last spark is flying,
　Still sweet to the end is my pet,
Who helps me, although she is dying,
　To light up a fresh cigarette!
　　　'T were better, etc.

THE BALLADE OF TOBACCO.

WHEN verdant youth sees life afar,
　　And first sets out wild oats to sow,
He puffs a stiff and stark cigar,
　　And quaffs champagne of Mumm & Co.
He likes not smoking yet; but though
　　Tobacco makes him sick indeed,
Cigars and wine he can't forego, —
　　A slave is each man to the weed.

In time his tastes more dainty are
　　And delicate.   Become a beau,
From out the country of the czar
　　He brings his cigarettes, and lo!
He sips the vintage of Bordeaux.
　　Thus keener relish shall succeed
The baser liking we outgrow, —
　　A slave is each man to the weed.

When age and his own lucky star
　　To him perfected wisdom show,
The schooner glides across the bar,
　　And beer for him shall freely flow;
A pipe with genial warmth shall glow,
　　To which he turns in direst need,
To seek in smoke surcease of woe, —
　　A slave is each man to the weed.

ENVOI.

Smokers, who doubt or con or pro,
    And ye who dare to drink, take heed!
And see in smoke a friendly foe, —
    A slave is each man to the weed.
                    BRANDER MATTHEWS.

HE RESPONDETH.

SHE.

YOU still persist in using,
        I observe with great regret,
The needlessly expensive
            Cigarette.

HE.

You should set a good example;
    But you seem to quite forget
That you use a thirty-dollar
            Vinaigrette.
                            Life.

TO SEE HER PIPE AWRY.

BETTY BOUNCER kept a stall
        At the corner of a street,
And she had a smile for all.
    Many were the friends she 'd **greet**
With kindly nod on passing by,
Who, smiling, saw her pipe awry.

Poor old lass! she loved her pipe,
    A constant friend it seemed to be;
As she sold her apples ripe,
    With an apple on each knee,
How she 'd make the smoke-wreaths fly,
As I 've watched her pipe awry!

Seasons came and seasons went,
    Only changing Betty's store;
Youngsters with her always spent
    Their little all and wished they 'd more:
Timidly with upturned eye
Staring at her pipe awry.

Bet was always at her post
    Early morn or even late;
Ginger beer or chestnut roast,
    Served she as she sat in state,
On two bushel-baskets high;
You should have seen her pipe awry!

Little care old Betty had,
    She quietly jogged on her way;
Never did her face look sad,
    Although she fumed the livelong day.
Guiltless seemed she of a sigh.
I never saw her pipe her eye!

                                    C. F.

INGIN SUMMER.

JEST about the time when Fall
    Gits to rattlin' in the trees,
An' the man thet knows it all,
    'Spicions frost in every breeze,
When a person tells hisse'f
    Thet the leaves look mighty thin,
Then thar blows a meller breaf!
    Ingin summer 's hyere agin.

Kind-uh smoky-lookin' blues
    Spins acrost the mountain-side,
An' the heavy mornin' dews
    Greens the grass up far an' wide,
Natur' raly 'pears as ef
    She wuz layin' off a day, —
Sort-uh drorin in her breaf
    'Fore she freezes up to stay.

Nary lick o' work I strike,
    'Long about this time of year!
I 'm a sort-uh slowly like,
    Right when Ingin summer 's here.
Wife and boys kin do the work;
    But a man with natchel wit,
Like I got, kin 'ford to shirk,
    Ef he has a turn for it.

Time when grapes set in to ripe,
    All I ast off any man
Is a common co'n-cob pipe
    With terbacker to my han';
Then jest loose me whar the air
    Simmers 'crost me, wahm an' free!
Promised lands ull find me thar;
    Wings ull fahly sprout on me!

I 'm a loungin' 'round on thrones,
    Bossin' worlds f'om shore to shore,
When I stretch my marrer-bones
    Jest outside the cabin door!
An' the sunshine peepin' down
    On my old head, bald an' gray,
'Pears right like the gilted crown,
    I expect to w'ar some day.

EVA WILDER MCGLASSON

EDIFYING REFLECTIONS OF A TOBAICO-SMOKER.

Set to music by Johann Sebastian Bach. Author unknown.
Translated by Edward Breck.

AS oft I fill my faithful pipe,
    To while away the moments glad,
With fragrant leaves, so rich and ripe,
    My mind perceives an image sad,
So that I can but clearly see
How very like it is to me.

My pipe is made of earth and clay,
From which my mortal part is wrought;
I, too, must turn to earth some day.
It often falls, as quick as thought,
And breaks in two, — puts out its flame;
My fate, alas! is but the same!

My pipe I color not, nor paint;
White it remains, and hence 't is true
That, when in Death's cold arms I faint,
My lips shall wear the ashen hue;
And as it blackens day by day,
So black the grave shall turn my clay!

And when the pipe is put alight
The smoke ascends, then trembles, wanes.
And soon dissolves in sunshine bright,
And but the whitened ash remains.
'T is so man's glory crumble must,
E'en as his body, into dust!

How oft the filler is mislaid;
And, rather than to seek in vain,
I use my finger in its stead,
And fancy as I feel the pain,
If coals can burn to such degree,
How hot, O Lord, must Hades be!

So in tobacco oft I find,
    Lessons of such instructive type;
And hence with calm, contented mind
    I live, and smoke my faithful pipe
In reverence where'er I roam, —
On land, on water, and at home.

THE LOST LOTUS.

'TIS said that in the sun-embroidered East,
    There dwelt a race whose softly flowing hours
Passed like the vision of a royal feast,
    By Nero given in the Baian bowers;
Thanks to the lotus-blossom spell,
Their lives were one long miracle.

In after years the passing sons of men
    Looked for those lotus blossoms all in vain,
Through every hillside, glade, and glen
    And e'en the isles of many a main;
Yet through the centuries some doom,
Forbade them see the lotus bloom.

The Old World wearied of the long pursuit,
    And called the sacred leaf a poet's theme,
When lo! the New World, rich in flower and fruit,
    Revealed the lotus, lovelier than the dream
That races of the long past days did haunt, —
The green-leaved, amber-tipped tobacco plant.

ANON.

THE SCENT OF A GOOD CIGAR.

WHAT is it comes through the deepening dusk, —
　　Something sweeter than jasmine scent,
Sweeter than rose and violet blent,
More potent in power than orange or musk?
The scent of a good cigar.

I am all alone in my quiet room,
And the windows are open wide and free
To let in the south wind's kiss for me,
While I rock in the softly gathering gloom,
And that subtle fragrance steals.

Just as a loving, tender hand
Will sometimes steal in yours,
It softly comes through the open doors,
And memory wakes at its command, —
The scent of that good cigar.

And what does it say?　Ah! that 's for me
And my heart alone to know;
But that heart thrills with a sudden glow,
Tears fill my eyes till I cannot see, —
From the scent of that good cigar.
　　　　　　　KATE A. CARRINGTON.

TO MY CIGAR.

YES, social friend, I love thee well,
    In learned doctor's spite;
Thy clouds all other clouds dispel,
    And lap me in delight.

What though they tell, with phizzes long,
    My years are sooner past!
I would reply with reason strong,
    They 're sweeter while they last.

When in the lonely evening hour,
    Attended but by thee,
O'er history's varied page I pore,
    Man's fate in thine I see.

Oft as the snowy column grows,
    Then breaks and falls away,
I trace how mighty realms thus rose,
    Thus tumbled to decay.

Awhile like thee earth's masters burn
    And smoke and fume around;
And then, like thee, to ashes turn,
    And mingle with the ground.

Life 's but a leaf adroitly rolled,
    And Time 's the wasting breath
That, late or early, we behold
    Gives all to dusty death.

From beggar's frieze to monarch's robe,
   One common doom is passed;
Sweet Nature's works, the swelling globe,
   Must all burn out at last.

And what is he who smokes thee now?
   A little moving heap,
That soon, like thee, to fate must bow,
   With thee in dust must sleep.

But though thy ashes downward go,
   Thy essence rolls on high;
Thus, when my body lieth low,
   My soul shall cleave the sky.
                CHARLES SPRAGUE.

KNICKERBOCKER.

SHADE of Herrick, Muse of Locker,
   Help me sing of Knickerbocker!
Boughton, had you bid me chant
Hymns to Peter Stuyvesant,
Had you bid me sing of Wouter,
He, the onion head, the doubter!
But to rhyme of this one — Mocker!
Who shall rhyme to Knickerbocker?
Nay, but where my hand must fail,
There the more shall yours avail;
You shall take your brush and paint
All that ring of figures quaint, —

All those Rip Van Winkle jokers,
All those solid-looking smokers,
Pulling at their pipes of amber,
In the dark-beamed Council Chamber.

Only art like yours can touch
Shapes so dignified — and Dutch;
Only art like yours can show
How the pine logs gleam and glow,
Till the firelight laughs and passes
'Twixt the tankards and the glasses,
Touching with responsive graces
All those grave Batavian faces,
Making bland and beatific
All that session soporific.

Then I come and write beneath:
Boughton, he deserves the wreath;
He can give us form and hue —
This the Muse can never do!

AUSTIN DOBSON

THE DISCOVERY OF TOBACCO.

A Sailor's Version.

THEY were three jolly sailors bold,
    Who sailed across the sea;
They 'd braved the storm, and stood the gale,
    And got to Virgin-ee.

'T was in the days of good Queen Bess, —
  Or p'raps a bit before, —
And now these here three sailors bold
  Went cruising on the shore.
A lurch to starboard, one to port,
  Now forrard, boys, go we,
With a haul and a " Ho ! " and a " That 's your sort ! "
  To find out Tobac-kee.

Says Jack, " This here 's a rummy land."
  Says Tom, " Well, shiver me !
The sun shines out as precious hot
  As ever I did see."
Says Dick, " Messmates, since here we be, " —
  And gave his eye a wink, —
" We 've come to find out Tobac-kee,
  Which means a drop to drink."

Says Jack, says he, " The Injins think — "
  Says Tom, " I 'll swear as they
Don't think at all."   Says Dick, " You 're right;
  It ain't their nat'ral way.
But I want to find out, my lads,
  This stuff of which they tell;
For if as it ain't meant to drink,
  Why, it must be meant to smell."

Says Tom, says he, " To drink or smell,
  I don't think this here 's meant."
Says Jack, says he, " Blame my old eyes,
  If I 'll believe it 's scent."

"Well, then," says Dick, "if that ain't square.
  It must be meant for meat;
So come along, my jovial mates,
  To find what 's good to eat."

They came across a great big plant,
  A-growing tall and true.
Says Jack, says he, " I 'm precious dry,"
  And picked a leaf to chew.
While Tom takes up a sun-dried bit,
  A-lying by the trees;
He rubs it in his hands to dust
  And then begins to sneeze.

Another leaf picks nimble Dick,
  And dries it in the sun,
And rolls it up all neat and tight.
  "My lads," says he, in fun,
" I mean to cook this precious weed."
  And then from out his poke
With burning-glass he lights the end,
  And quick blows up the smoke.

Says Jack, says he, "Of Paradise
  I 've heerd some people tell."
Says Tom, says he, "This here will do;
  Let 's have another smell."
Says Dick, his face all pleasant smiles,
  A-looking through a cloud,
" It strikes me here 's the cap'en bold,
  And now we 'll all be rowed."

Up comes brave Hawkins on the beach ;
  " Shiver my hull ! " he cries,
" What 's these here games, my merry men ? "
  And then, " Why, blame my eyes !
Here 's one as chaws, and one as snuffs,
  And t' other of the three
Is smoking like a chimbley-pot —
  They 've found out Tobac-kee ! "

So if ever you should hear
  Of Raleigh, and them lies
About his sarvant and his pipe
  And him as " Fire ! " cries,
You say as 't was three sailors bold
  As sailed to Virgin-ee
In brave old Hawkins' gallant ship
  Who found out Tobac-kee.
A lurch to starboard, one to port,
  Now forrard, boys, go we,
With a haul and a " Ho ! " and a " That 's your
    sort ! "
  To find out Tobac-kee.

                    Cigar and Tobacco World, London.

"KEATS TOOK SNUFF."

" Keats took snuff. . . . It has been established by the praise-
worthy editorial research of Mr. Burton Forman."

So "Keats took snuff?"   A few more years,
    When we are dead and famous — eh?
Will they record our pipes and beers,
    And if we smoked cigars or clay?
Or will the world cry "Quantum suff"
To tattle such as "Keats took snuff"?

Perhaps some chronicler would wish
    To know what whiskey we preferred,
And if we ever dined on fish,
    Or only took the joint and bird.
Such facts are quite as worthy stuff,
Good chronicler, as "Keats took snuff."

You answer: "But, if you were Keats — "
    Tut! never mind your buts and ifs,
Of little men record their meats,
    Their drinks, their troubles, and their tiffs.
Of the great dead there 's gold enough
To spare us such as "Keats took snuff."

Well, go your ways, you little folk,
  Who polish up the great folk's lives;
Record the follies that they spoke,
  And paint their squabbles with their wives.
Somewhere, if ever ghosts be gruff,
I trust some Keats will "give you snuff."

                                        The Globe, London.

THE BALLAD OF THE PIPE.

OH, give me but Virginia's weed,
    An earthen bowl, a stem of reed,
  What care I for the weather?
Though winter freeze and summer broil
We rest us from our days of toil
  My Pipe and I together!

Like to a priest of sacred fane,
I nightly light the glow again
  With reverence and pleasure;
For through this plain and modest bowl
I coax sweet mem'ry to my soul
  And many trippings measure!

There 's comfort in each puff of smoke,
Defiance to ill-fortune's stroke
  And happiness forever!
There grows a volume full of thought
And humor, than the book you bought
  Holds nothing half so clever!

The summer fragrance, all pent up
Among the leaves, is here sent up
   In dreams of summer glory;
And these blue clouds that slowly rise
Were colored by the summer skies,
   And tell a summer story.

And oh ! the happiest, sweetest times
Come ringing all their silver chimes
   Of merry songs and laughter;
And all that may be well and worth
For Mother Future to bring forth
   I do imagine after.

What care I if my poor means
Clad not my walls with splendid scenes
   And pictures by the masters;
Here in the curling smoke-wreath glow
Bold hills and lovely vales below,
   And brooks with nodding asters.

All that on earth is fair and fine,
This fragrant magic makes it mine,
   And gives me sole dominion;
And if you call me fanciful,
I only take a stronger pull,
   And laugh at your opinion.

Let others fret and fume with care,
'T is easy finding everywhere,
   But happiness is rarer;

And if I find it sweet and ripe,
In this tobacco and my pipe,
   I 'll count it all the fairer.

Then give me but Virginia's weed,
An earthen bowl, a stem of reed,
   What care I for the weather?
Though winter freeze, or summer broil
We rest us from the days of toil,
   My Pipe and I together.

HERMANN RAVE.

THE OLD CLAY PIPE.

THERE 'S a lot of solid comfort
   In an old clay pipe, I find,
If you 're kind of out of humor
   Or in trouble in your mind.
When you 're feeling awful lonesome
   And don't know just what to do,
There 's a heap of satisfaction
   If you smoke a pipe or two.

The ten thousand pleasant memories
   That are buried in your soul
Are playing hide and seek with you
   Around that smoking bowl.
These are mighty restful moments:
   You 're at peace with all the world,
And the panorama changes
   As the thin blue smoke is curled.

Now you cross the bridge of sorrows,
  Now you enter pleasant lands,
And before an open doorway,
  You will linger to shake hands
With a lithe and girlish figure
  That is coming through the door;
Ah! you recognize the features:
  You have seen that face before.

You are at the dear old homestead
  Where you spent those happy years;
You are romping with the children;
  You are smiling through your tears;
You have fought and whipped the bully
  You are eight and he is ten.
Oh! how rapidly we travel, —
  You are now a boy again.

You approach the open doorway,
  And before the old armchair
You will stop and kiss the grandma,
  You will smooth the thin white hair;
You will read the open Bible,
  For the lamp is lit, you see.
It is now your hour for bed-time
  And you kneel at mother's knee.

Still you linger at the hearthstone;
  You are loath to leave the place,
When an apple cut 's in progress;
  You must wait and dance with Grace.

What's the matter with the music?
  Only this: The pipe is broke,
And a thousand pleasant fancies
  Vanish promptly with the smoke.

              A. B. VAN FLEET.

PERNICIOUS WEED!

THE pipe, with solemn interposing puff,
  Makes half a sentence at a time enough;
The dozing sages drop the drowsy strain,
Then pause and puff, and speak, and pause again.
Such often, like the tube they so admire,
Important triflers! have more smoke than fire.
Pernicious weed! whose scent the fair annoys,
Unfriendly to society's chief joys,
Thy worst effect is banishing for hours
The sex whose presence civilizes ours.

              WILLIAM COWPER.

TWO OTHER HEARTS.

FULL tender beamed the light of love down from
  his manly face,
As he pressed her to his bosom in a fervent, fond
  embrace.
No cost of others' happiness found place within his
  thought;
The weakness of life's brittle thread no dim forebod-
  ings brought.

But tenderer than the light of love, more brittle than
  life's thread,
The shrouds that wrapped two other hearts gave up
  their withered dead;
For, crumbling in his waistcoat, their glowing future
  dashed,
Two excellent Havanas were very badly smashed.

London Tobacco.

THE SMOKE TRAVELLER.

WHEN I puff my cigarette,
  Straight I see a Spanish girl, —
Mantilla, fan, coquettish curl,
Languid airs and dimpled face,
Calculating, fatal grace;
Hear a twittering serenade
Under lofty balcony played;
Queen at bull-fight, naught she cares
What her agile lover dares;
She can love and quick forget.

Let me but my meerschaum light,
  I behold a bearded man,
  Built upon capacious plan,
Sabre-slashed in war or duel,
Gruff of aspect, but not cruel,
Metaphysically muddled,

With strong beer a little fuddled,
  Slow in love, and deep in books,
  More sentimental than he looks,
Swears new friendships every night.

Let me my chibouk enkindle, —
  In a tent I 'm quick set down
  With a Bedouin, lean and brown,
  Plotting gain of merchandise,
  Or perchance of robber prize ;
  Clumsy camel load upheaving,
  Woman deftly carpet-weaving,
  Meal of dates and bread and salt,
  While in azure heavenly vault
Throbbing stars begin to dwindle.

Glowing coal in clay dudheen
  Carries me to sweet Killarney,
  Full of hypocritic blarney. —
  Huts with babies, pigs, and hens
  Mixed together, bogs and fens,
  Shillalahs, praties, usquebaugh,
  Tenants defying hated law,
  Fair blue eyes with lashes black,
  Eyes black and blue from cudgel-thwack, —
So fair, so foul, is Erin green.

My nargileh once inflamed,
  Quick appears a Turk with turban,
  Girt with guards in palace urban,
  Or in house by summer sea

Slave-girls dancing languidly,
Bow-string, sack, and bastinado,
Black boats darting in the shadow;
Let things happen as they please,
Whether well or ill at ease,
Fate alone is blessed or blamed.

With my ancient calumet
I can raise a wigwam's smoke,
And the copper tribe invoke, —
Scalps and wampum, bows and knives,
Slender maidens, greasy wives,
Papoose hanging on a tree,
Chieftains squatting silently,
Feathers, beads, and hideous paint,
Medicine-man and wooden-saint, —
Forest-framed the vision set.

My cigar breeds many forms, —
Planter of the rich Havana
Mopping brow with sheer bandanna,
Russian prince in fur arrayed,
Paris fop on dress parade,
London swell just after dinner,
Wall Street broker — gambling sinner!
Delver in Nevada mine,
Scotch laird bawling " Auld Lang Syne."
Thus Raleigh's weed my fancy warms.

Life's review in smoke goes past, —
Fickle fortune, stubborn fate,
Right discovered all too late,

Beings loved and gone before,
Beings loved but friends no more,
Self-reproach and futile sighs,
Vanity in birth that dies,
Longing, heart-break, adoration,—
Nothing sure in expectation
Save ash-receiver at the last.

Irving Browne.

SMOKING SONG.

WITH grateful twirl our smoke-wreaths curl,
    As mist from the waterfall given,
Or the locks that float round beauty's throat
  In the whispering air of even.

Chorus. Then drown the fears of the coming years,
        And the dread of change before us;
      The way is sweet to our willing feet,
        With the smoke-wreaths twining o'er us.

As the light beams through the ringlets blue,
  Will hope beam through our sorrow,
While the gathering wreath of the smoke we breathe
  Shuts out the fear of to-morrow.

A magic charm in the evening calm
  Calls thought from mem'ry's treasure;
But clear and bright in the liquid light
  Are the smoke-called dreams of pleasure.

Then who shall chide, with boasting **pride,**
    Delights they ne'er have tasted?
Oh, let them smile while we beguile
    The hour with joys they 've wasted.

College Song.

HOW IT ONCE WAS.

RIGHT stout and strong the worthy burghers
        stood,
        Or rather, sat,
Drank beer in plenty, ate abundant food;
For they to ancient customs still were true,
And smoked, and smoked, because they surely knew
        What they were at.

William the Testy ruled New Amsterdam, —
        A tall man he, —
Whose rule was meant by him to be no sham,
But rather like the stern paternal style
That sways the city now.   He made the while
        A rough decree.

He ordered that the pipes should cease to smoke,
        From that day on.
The people took the order as a joke;
They did not think, who smoked from childhood up,
That one man such delight would seek to stop,
        Even in fun.

But when at last it dawned upon their minds
      That this was meant,
They closed their houses, shut their window blinds,
Brought forth tobacco from their ample hoard,
And to the governor's house with one accord
      The burghers went.

They carried chairs, and sat without a word
      Before his porch,
And smoked, and smoked, and not a sound was heard,
Till Kieft came forth to take the morning air,
With speech that would have burned them then and
    there
      If words could scorch.

But they, however savagely he spoke,
      Made no reply.
Higher and thicker rose the clouds of smoke,
And Kieft, perceiving that they would be free
Tried not to put in force his harsh decree,
      But let it die.

              New York Sun.

HER BROTHER'S CIGARETTE.

LIKE raven's wings her locks of jet,
    Her soft eyes touched with fond regret,
Doubt and desire her mind beset,
Fondling her brother's cigarette.

Roses with dewy diamonds set,
Drooped o'er the window's parapet;
With grace she turned a match to get,
And lit her brother's cigarette.

Her puffs of smoky violet
Twined in fantastic silhouette;
She blushed, laughed, coughed a little, yet,
She smoked her brother's cigarette.

Her eyes with briny tears were wet,
Her bang grew limp beneath its net,
Her brow was gemmed with beaded sweat,
And to her bed she went, you bet.

ANON.

IN THE OL' TOBACKER PATCH.

I JESS kind o' feel so lonesome that I don't know
    what to do,
  When I think about them days we used to spend
A hoein' out tobacker in th' clearin' — me an' you —
  An' a wishin' that the day was at an end.
For the dewdrops was a sparklin' on the beeches'
    tender leaves
  As we started out a workin' in the morn;
An' th' noonday sun was sendin' down a shower of
    burnin' sheaves
  When we heard the welcome-soundin' dinner-horn.

An' th' shadders round us gathered in a sort of
    ghostly batch,
'Fore we started home from workin' in that ol'
    tobacker patch.

I 'm a feelin' mighty lonesome, as I look aroun' to-
    day,
    For I see th' change that 's taken place since then.
All th' hills is brown and faded, for th' woods is
    cleared away ;
    You an' me has changed from ragged boys to men ;
You are livin' in th' city that we ust to dream about ;
    I am still a dwellin' here upon the place,
But my form is bent an' feeble, which was once so
    straight and stout,
    An' there 's most a thousand wrinkles on my face.
You have made a mint of money ; I, perhaps have
    been your match,
But we both enjoyed life better in that ol' tobacker
    patch.

S. Q. LAPIUS.

MÆCENAS BIDS HIS FRIEND TO DINE.

I BEG you come to-night and dine.
    A welcome waits you, and sound wine, —
The Roederer chilly to a charm,
As Juno's breath the claret warm,
The sherry of an ancient brand.

No Persian pomp, you understand, —
A soup, a fish, two meats, and then
A salad fit for aldermen
(When aldermen, alas the days !
Were really worth their *mayonnaise*);
A dish of grapes whose clusters won
Their bronze in Carolinian sun ;
Next, cheese — for you the Neufchâtel,
A bit of Cheshire likes me well ;
Café au lait or coffee black,
With Kirsch or Kümmel or cognac
(The German band in Irving Place
By this time purple in the face) ;
Cigars and pipes.   These being through,
Friends shall drop in, a very few —
Shakespeare and Milton, and no more.
When these are guests I bolt the door,
With " Not at home " to any one
Excepting Alfred Tennyson.

ANON.

TO MY MEERSCHAUM.

THERE 'S a charm in the sun-crested hills,
    In the quivering light of a star,
In the flash of a silvery rill,
    Yet to me thou art lovelier far,
            My Meerschaum !

There 's a love in her witching dark eye,
  There 's a love in her tresses at play,
Yet her love would be worth not a sigh,
  If from thee she could lure me away,
                My Meerschaum !

Let revellers sing of their wine,
  As they toss it in ecstasy down,
But the bowl I call for is thine,
  With its deepening amber and brown,
                My Meerschaum !

For when trouble would bid me despair,
  I call for a flagon of beer,
And puff a defiance to care,
  Till sorrows in smoke disappear,
                My Meerschaum!

Though mid pleasures unnumbered I whirl,
  Though I traverse the billowy sea,
Yet the waving and beautiful curl
  Of thy smoke 's ever dearer to me,
                My Meerschaum !
                    P. D. R.

OLD PIPE OF MINE.

COMPANION of my lonely hours,
  Full many a time 'twixt night and morn
Thy muse hath roamed through poesy's bowers
  Upon thy fragrant pinions borne.

Let others seek the bliss that reigns
　　In homage paid at beauty's shrine,
We envy not such foolish gains,
　　In sweet content, old pipe of mine.

Ah! you have been a travelled pipe;
　　But now, of course, you 're getting stale,
Just like myself, and rather ripe;
　　You 've had your fill of cakes and ale,
And half-forgotten memories, too.
　　And all the pensive thoughts that twine
Around a past that, *entre nous*,
　　Has pleasant been, old pipe of mine.

Old pipe of mine, for many a year
　　What boon companions we have been!
With here a smile and there a tear,
　　How many changes we have seen!
How many hearts have ceased to beat,
　　How many eyes have ceased to shine,
How many friends will never meet,
　　Since first we met, old pipe of mine!

Though here and there the road was deep,
　　And now and then the rain would fall;
We managed every time to keep
　　A sturdy forehead to them all!
And even when she left my side,
　　We did n't wait to fret or pine,
Oh, no; we said the world was wide,
　　And luck would turn, old pipe of mine!

And it has turned since you and I
   Set out to face the world alone;
And, in a garret near the sky,
   Had scarce a crust to call our own,
But many a banquet, Barmecide;
   And many a dream of hope divine,
Lie buried in the moaning tide,
   That drowns the past, old pipe of mine!

.   .   .   .

But prosing is n't quite the thing,
   And so, I guess, I 'll give it up:
Just wait a moment while I sing;
   We 'll have another parting cup,
And then to bed.   The stars are low;
   Yon sickly moon has ceased to shine;
So here she goes, and off we go
   To Slumberland, old pipe of mine!

JOHN J. GORMLEY.

CANNON SONG.

COME, seniors, come, and fill your pipes,
   Your richest incense raise;
Let 's take a smoke, a parting smoke,
   For good old by-gone days!

Chorus.   For good old by-gone days,
      We 'll smoke for good old by-gone days!
      We 'll take a smoke, a parting smoke,
         For good old by-gone days!

We 'll crown the cannon with a cloud,
 We 'll celebrate its praise;
Recalling *its* old parting smoke,
 For good old by-gone days!

We 'll smoke to these we leave behind
 In devious college ways;
We 'll smoke to songs we 've sung before,
 In good old by-gone days.

We 'll smoke to *Alma Mater's* name;
 She loves the cloud we raise!
For well she knows the " biggest guns "
 Are in the coming days!

We 'll smoke the times, the good old times,
 When we were called to *fire!*
Their light shall blaze in memory,
 Till the lamp of life expire!

Then let each smoking pipe be broke, —
 Hurrah for coming days!
We 'll take a march, a merry march,
 To meet the coming days!

H. P. PECK.

TOBACCO.

THE Indian weed, withered quite,
 Green at noon, cut down at night,
Shows thy decay; all flesh is hay,
Thus thinke, then drinke tobacco.

The pipe that is so lily-white,
Shows thee to be a mortal wight;
And even such, gone with a touch,
Thus thinke, then drinke tobacco.

And when the smoke ascends on high,
Thinke thou beholdst the vanity
Of worldly stuffe, gone with a puffe,
Thus thinke, then drinke tobacco.

And when the pipe grows foal within,
Think on thy soule defil'd with sin,
And then the fire it doth require.
Thus thinke, then drinke tobacco.

The ashes that are left behind,
May serve to put thee still in mind,
That unto dust return thou must.
Thus thinke, then drinke tobacco.

GEORGE WITHER, 1620.

VIRGINIA'S KINGLY PLANT.

By an " Old Sait."

OH, muse! grant me the power
(I have the will) to sing
How oft in lonely hour,
When storms would round me lower,
Tobacco 's proved a king!

Philanthropists, no doubt
With good intentions ripe,
Their dogmas may put out,
And arrogantly shout
The evils of the pipe.

Kind moralists, with tracts,
Opinions fine may show ;
Produce a thousand facts, —
How ill tobacco acts
Man's system to o'erthrow.

Learn'd doctors have employed
Much patience, time, and skill,
To prove tobacco cloyed
With acrid alkaloid,
With power the nerves to kill.

E'en popes have curst the plant;
Kings bade its use to cease;
But all the pontiff's rant
And royal James's cant
Ne'er made its use decrease.

Teetotalers may stamp
And roar at pipes and beer;
But place them in a swamp,
When nights are dark and damp, —
Their tunes would change, I fear.

No advocate am I
Of excess in one or t' other,
And ne'er essayed to try
In wine to drown a sigh,
Or a single care to smother.

Yet, in moderation pure,
A glass is well enough;
But a troubled heart to cure,
Kind feelings to insure,
Give me a cheerful puff.

How oft a learn'd divine
His sermons will prepare,
Not by imbibing wine,
But 'neath th' influence fine
Of a pipe of "baccy" rare!

How many a pleasing scene,
How many a happy joke,
How many a satire keen,
Or problem sharp, has been
Evolved or born of smoke!

How oft amidst the jar,
Of storms on ruin bent,
On shipboard, near or far,
To the drenched and shiv'ring tar,
Tobacco's solace lent!

Oh, tell me not 't is bad,
Or that it shortens life!
Its charms can soothe the sad,
And make the wretched glad,
In trouble and in strife.

'T is used in every clime,
By all men, high and low;
It is praised in prose and rhyme,
And can but end with time;
So let the kind herb grow!

'T is a friend to the distress'd;
'T is a comforter in need;
It is social, soothing, blest;
It has fragrance, force, and zest;
Then hail the kingly weed!

ANON.

TOO GREAT A SACRIFICE.

THE maid, as by the papers doth appear,
  Whom fifty thousand dollars made so dear,
To test Lothario's passion, simply said,
"Forego the weed before we go to wed.
For smoke, take flame; I'll be that flame's bright
    fanner.
To have your Anna, give up your Havana."
But he, when thus she brought him to the scratch,
Lit his cigar, and threw away his match.

ANON.

TO A PIPE OF TOBACCO.

COME, lovely tube, by friendship blest,
　Belov'd and honored by the wise,
Come filled with honest " Weekly's best,"
　And kindled from the lofty skies.

While round me clouds of incense roll,
　With guiltless joys you charm the sense,
And nobler pleasure to the soul
　In hints of moral truth dispense.

Soon as you feel th' enliv'ning ray,
　To dust you hasten to return,
And teach me that my earliest day
　Began to give me to the urn.

But though thy grosser substance sink
　To dust, thy purer part aspires;
This when I see, I joy to think
　That earth but half of me requires.

Like thee, myself am born to die,
　Made half to rise, and half to fall.
Oh, could I, while my moments fly,
　The bliss you give me give to all!
　　　　　Gentleman's Magazine, July, 1745.

IN the smoke of my dear cigarito
   Cloud castles rise gorgeous and tall;
And Eros, divine muchachito,
   With smiles hovers over it all.

But dreaming, forgetting to cherish
   The fire at my lips as it dies,
The dream and the rapture must perish,
   And Eros descend from the skies.

O wicked and false muchachito,
   Your rapture I yet may recall;
But, like my re-lit cigarito,
   A bitterness tinges it all.

                  CAMILLA K. VON K.

A GOOD CIGAR.

OH, 't is well and enough,
   A whiff or a puff
From the heart of a pipe to get;
  And a dainty maid
  Or a budding blade
May toy with the cigarette;
  But a man, when the time
  Of a glorious prime
Dawns forth like a morning star,
  Wants the dark-brown bloom
  And the sweet perfume
That go with a good cigar.

To lazily float
In a painted boat
On a shimmering morning sea.
Or to flirt with a maid
In the afternoon shade
Seems good enough sport to be;
But the evening hour,
With its subtle power,
Is sweeter and better far,
If joined to the joy,
Devoid of alloy,
That lurks in a good cigar.

When a blanket wet
Is solidly set
O'er hopes prematurely grown;
When ambition is tame,
And energy lame,
And the bloom from the fruit is blown;
When to dance and to dine
With women and wine
Past poverty pleasures are, —
A man's not bereft
Of all peace, if there's left
The joy of a good cigar.

NORRIS BULL.

A GLASS is good, and a lass is good,
    And a pipe to smoke in cold weather;
The world is good, and the people are good,
    And we're all good fellows together.

JOHN O'KEEFE: *Sprigs of Laurel,*
                            Act ii. sc. i.

MY FRIENDLY PIPE.

LET sybarites still dream delights
    While smoking cigarettes,
Whose opiates get in their pates
    Till waking brings regrets;
Oh, let them doze, devoid of woes,
    Of troubles, and of frets.

And let the chap who loves to nap
    With his cigar in hand
Pursue his way, and live his day,
    As runs time's changing sand;
Let him delight by day and night
    In his peculiar brand.

But as for me, I love to be
    Provided with a pipe, —
A rare old bowl to warm my soul,
    A meerschaum brown and ripe, —
With good plug cut, no stump or butt,
    Nor filthy gutter-snipe.

My joys increase !   It brings me peace
    As nothing else can do ;
From all the strife of daily life
    Here my relief is true.
I watch its rings ; it purrs and sings —
    And then it 's cheaper, too !

                  Detroit Tribune.

ODE TO TOBACCO.

COME then, Tobacco, new-found friend,
    Come, and thy suppliant attend
      In each dull, lonely hour ;
And though misfortunes lie around,
Thicker than hailstones on the ground,
      I 'll rest upon thy power.
Then while the coxcomb, pert and proud,
The politician, learned and loud,
      Keep one eternal clack,
I 'll tread where silent Nature smiles,
Where Solitude our woe beguiles,
      And chew thee, dear Tobac.

                  Daniel Webster.

A BACHELOR'S SOLILOQUY.

I SIT all alone with my pipe by the fire,
    I ne'er knew the Benedict's yoke ;
I worship a fairy-like, fanciful form,
    That goes up the chimney in smoke.

I sit in my dressing-gowned slipperful ease,
    Without wife or bairns to provoke,
And puff at my pipe, while my hopes and my fears
    All go up the chimney in smoke.

I sit with my pipe, and my heart's lonesome care
    I try, but all vainly, to choke.
Ah, me! but I find that the flame that Love lights
    Won't go up the chimney in smoke.

    Cigar and Tobacco World, London.

THE DREAMER'S PIPE.

MEERSCHAUM, thing with amber tip,
    Clutched between the dreamer's lip,
Fragrant odors from thy bowl
Mingling with the dreamer's soul;
Curling wreaths of smoke ascending,
Comfort sweet with incense blending.
Joy and peace and solace sending
    To the dreamer's heart.

Fashioned like a satyr's head,
Crowned with fire, glowing red,
Quaintly carved and softly sleek
As Afric maiden's downy cheek.
Comrade of each idle hour
In forest shade or leafy bower;
Lotus-eaters from thy power
    Ne'er can break apart.

Darkly colored from long use
With tobacco's balmy juice
From snowy white to ebon turned
By the incense daily burned.
Laid at night within thy case
Of velvet soft — thy resting place —
Whence with leering, stained face
    Daily thou must start, —

To soothe the dreamer's every care,
To glow and burn and fill the air
With thy curling perfume rare;
As thou charmest gloom away,
With the dreamer rest for aye
Friend of youth, and manhood ripe
All hail to thee, thou meerschaum pipe!
        New Orleans Times Democrat.

SUBLIME TOBACCO.

BUT here the herald of the self-same mouth
    Came breathing o'er the aromatic South,
Not like a " bed of violets " on the gale,
But such as wafts its cloud o'er grog or ale,
Borne from a short, frail pipe, which yet had blown
Its gentle odors over either zone,
And, puff'd where'er minds rise or waters roll,
Had wafted smoke from Portsmouth to the Pole,
Opposed its vapor as the lightning flash'd,
And reek'd, 'midst mountain billows unabashed,

To Æolus a constant sacrifice,
Through every change of all the varying skies.
And what was he who bore it? I may err,
But deem him sailor or philosopher.
Sublime tobacco! which from east to west
Cheers the tar's labor or the Turkman's rest;
Which on the Moslem's ottoman divides
His hours, and rivals opiums and his brides;
Magnificent in Stamboul, but less grand,
Though not less loved, in Wapping on the Strand;
Divine in hookas, glorious in a pipe,
When tipp'd with amber, mellow, rich, and ripe;
Like other charmers, wooing the caress
More dazzlingly when daring in full dress;
Yet thy true lovers more admire by far
Thy naked beauties, — give me a cigar!

LORD BYRON:
The Island, Canto ii., Stanza 19.

SMOKING AWAY.

FLOATING away like the fountains' spray,
    Or the snow-white plume of a maiden,
The smoke-wreaths rise to the starlit skies
    With blissful fragrance laden.

Chorus.   Then smoke away till a golden ray
        Lights up the dawn of the morrow,
    For a cheerful cigar, like a shield, will bar,
        The blows of care and sorrow.

The leaf burns bright, like the gems of light
   That flash in the braids of Beauty;
It nerves each heart for the hero's part
   On the battle-plain of duty.

In the thoughtful gloom of his darkened room,
   Sits the child of song and story,
But his heart is light, for his pipe burns bright,
   And his dreams are all of glory.

By the blazing fire sits the gray-haired sire,
   And infant arms surround him;
And he smiles on all in that quaint old hall,
   While the smoke-curls float around him.

In the forest grand of our native land,
   When the savage conflict ended,
The "pipe of peace" brought a sweet release
   From toil and terror blended.

The dark-eyed train of the maids of Spain
   'Neath their arbor shades trip lightly,
And a gleaming cigar, like a new-born star,
   In the clasp of their lips burns brightly.

It warms the soul like the blushing bowl,
   With its rose-red burden streaming,
And drowns it in bliss, like the first warm kiss
   From the lips with love-buds teeming.

                FRANCIS MILES FINCH.

A FAREWELL TO TOBACCO.

MAY the Babylonish curse
    Straight confound my stammering verse
If I can a passage see
In this word-perplexity,
Or a fit expression find,
Or a language to my mind
(Still the phrase is wide or scant),
To take leave of thee, GREAT PLANT!
Or in any terms relate
Half my love, or half my hate:
For I hate, yet love, thee so,
That, whichever thing I show,
The plain truth will seem to be
A constrain'd hyperbole,
And the passion to proceed
More from a mistress than a weed.

  Sooty retainer to the vine,
Bacchus' black servant, negro fine;
Sorcerer, that mak'st us dote upon
Thy begrimed complexion,
And, for thy pernicious sake,
More and greater oaths to break
Than reclaimèd lovers take
'Gainst women: thou thy siege dost lay
Much too in the female way,
While thou suck'st the lab'ring breath
Faster than kisses or than death.

Thou in such a cloud dost bind us,
That our worst foes cannot find us,
And ill-fortune, that would thwart us,
Shoots at rovers, shooting at us;
While each man, through thy height'ning steam
Does like a smoking Etna seem,
And all about us does express
(Fancy and wit in richest dress)
A Sicilian fruitfulness.

Thou through such a mist dost show us,
That our best friends do not know us,
And, for those allowèd features,
Due to reasonable creatures,
Liken'st us to fell Chimeras,
Monsters that, who see us, fear us;
Worse than Cerberus or Geryon,
Or, who first loved a cloud, Ixion.

Bacchus we know, and we allow
His tipsy rites.   But what art thou,
That but by reflex canst show
What his deity can do,
As the false Egyptian spell
Aped the true Hebrew miracle,
Some few vapors thou mayst raise
The weak brain may serve to amaze,
But to the reins and nobler heart
Canst nor life nor heat impart.

Brother of Bacchus, later born,
The Old World was sure forlorn
Wanting thee, that aidest more
The god's victories than before
All his panthers, and the brawls
Of his piping Bacchanals.
These, as stale, we disallow,
Or judge of *thee* meant ; only thou
His true Indian conquest art;
And for ivy round his dart
The reformèd god now weaves
A finer thyrsus of thy leaves.

Scent to match thy rich perfume
Chemic art did ne'er presume,
Through her quaint alembic strain,
None so sov'reign to the brain.
Nature, that did in thee excel,
Framed again no second smell.
Roses, violets, but toys
For the smaller sort of boys,
Or for greener damsels meant;
Thou art the only manly scent.

Stinking'st of the stinking kind,
Filth of the mouth and fog of the mind,
Africa, that brags her foison,
Breeds no such prodigious poison,
Henbane, nightshade, both together,
Hemlock, aconite —

> Nay, rather,
Plant divine, of rarest virtue;
Blisters on the tongue would hurt you.
'T was but in a sort I blamed thee;
None e'er prosper'd who defamed thee;
Irony all, and feign'd abuse,
Such as perplex'd lovers use
At a need when, in despair
To paint forth their fairest fair,
Or in part but to express
That exceeding comeliness
Which their fancies doth so strike,
They borrow language of dislike;
And, instead of Dearest Miss,
Jewel, Honey, Sweetheart, Bliss,
And those forms of old admiring,
Call her Cockatrice and Siren,
Basilisk, and all that 's evil,
Witch, Hyena, Mermaid, Devil,
Ethiop, Wench, and Blackamore,
Monkey, Ape, and twenty more,
Friendly Trait'ress, loving Foe, —
Not that she is truly so,
But no other way they know
A contentment to express,
Borders so upon excess
That they do not rightly wot
Whether it be pain or not.

Or as men, constrain'd to part
With what 's nearest to their heart,

While their sorrow 's at the height
Lose discrimination quite,
And their hasty wrath let fall,
To appease their frantic gall,
On the darling thing whatever
Whence they feel it death to sever,
Though it be, as they, perforce,
Guiltless of the sad divorce.

For I must (nor let it grieve thee,
Friendliest of plants, that I must) leave thee.
For thy sake, TOBACCO, I
Would do anything but die,
And but seek to extend my days
Long enough to sing thy praise.
But as she who once hath been
A king's consort is a queen
Ever after, nor will bate
Any tittle of her state,
Though a widow or divorced,
So I, from thy converse forced,
The old name and style retain,
A right Katherine of Spain;
And a seat, too, 'mongst the joys
Of the blest Tobacco Boys,
Where, though I by sour physician
Am debarr'd the full fruition
Of thy favors, I may catch
Some collateral sweets, and snatch
Sidelong odors, that give life
Like glances from a neighbor's wife,

And still live in the by-places
And the suburbs of thy graces,
And in thy borders take delight,
An unconquer'd Canaanite.

CHARLES LAMB.

A WINTER EVENING HYMN TO MY FIRE

NICOTIA, dearer to the Muse
  Than all the grape's bewildering juice,
We worship, unforbid of thee;
And as her incense floats and curls
In airy spires and wayward whirls,
Or poises on its tremulous stalk
A flower of frailest reverie,
So winds and loiters, idly free,
The current of unguided talk,
Now laughter-rippled, and now caught
In smooth dark pools of deeper thought.
Meanwhile thou mellowest every word,
A sweetly unobtrusive third;
For thou hast magic beyond wine
To unlock natures each to each;
The unspoken thought thou canst divine;
Thou fill'st the pauses of the speech
With whispers that to dreamland reach,
And frozen fancy-springs unchain
In Arctic outskirts of the brain.
Sun of all inmost confidences,

To thy rays doth the heart unclose
Its formal calyx of pretences,
That close against rude day's offences,
And open its shy midnight rose!

JAMES RUSSELL LOWELL.

MY PIPE AND I.

THERE may be comrades in this world,
   As stanch and true as steel.
There are: and by their friendships firm
   Is life made only real.
But, after all, of all these hearts
   That close with mine entwine,
None lie so near, nor seem so dear
   As this old pipe of mine.

My silent friend — whose voice is held
   Fast for my ear alone —
Stays with me always, well content,
   With Darby to be Joan.
No fickleness disturbs our lot;
   No jars its peace to smother;
Ah, no; my faithful pipe and I
   Have wooed and won — each other.

On clouds of curling incense sweet,
   We go — my pipe and I —
To lands far off, where skies stay blue
   Through all the years that fly.

And nights and days, with rosy dreams
  Teems bright — an endless throng
That passing leave, in echoing wake,
  Soft murmurings of song.

Does this dream fade?   Another comes
  To fill its place and more.
In castles silvern roam we now,
  They 're ours!   All!   All are ours!
What'er the wreathing rings enfold
  Drops shimmering golden showers!

No sordid cost our steps can stay,
  We travel free as air.
Our wings are fancies, incense-borne,
  That feather-light upbear.
Begone! ye powers of steam and flood,
  Thy roads creep far too slow;
We need thee not.   My pipe and I
  Swifter than Time must go.

Why, what is this?   The pipe gone out?
  Well, well, the fire 's out, too!
The dreams are gone — we 're poor once more;
  Life's pain begins anew.
'T is time for sleep, my faithful pipe,
  But may thy dreamings be,
Through slumbering hours hued as bright
  As those thou gav'st to me!

                    ELTON J. BUCKLEY.

SIC TRANSIT.

JUST a note that I found on my table,
  By the bills of a year buried o'er,
In a feminine hand and requesting
  My presence for tennis at four.

Half remorseful for leaving it lying
  In surroundings unworthy as those,
I carefully dusted and smoothed it,
  And mutely begged pardon of Rose.

But I thought with a smile of the proverb
  Which says you may treat as you will
The vase which has once contained roses,
  Their fragrance will cling to it still.

For the writer I scarcely remember,
  The occasion has vanished afar,
And the fragrance that clings to the letter
  Recalls — an Havana cigar.

W. B. ANDERSON.

THE BETROTHED.

"You must choose between me and your cigar."

OPEN the old cigar-box, get me a Cuba stout,
  For things are running crossways, and Maggie
    and I are out.

We quarrelled about Havanas — we fought o'er a
    good cheroot,
And I know she is exacting, and she says I am a
    brute.

Open the old cigar-box — let me consider a space;
In the soft blue veil of the vapor, musing on Maggie's
    face.

Maggie is pretty to look at, — Maggie 's a loving lass,
But the prettiest cheeks must wrinkle, the truest of
    loves must pass.

There's peace in a Laranaga, there 's calm in a Henry
    Clay,
But the best cigar in an hour is finished and thrown
    away, —

Thrown away for another as perfect and ripe and
    brown, —
But I could not throw away Maggie for fear o' the
    talk o' the town !

Maggie my wife at fifty, — gray and dour and old, —
With never another Maggie to purchase for love or
    gold !

And the light of Days that have Been the dark of the
    Days that Are,
And Love's torch stinking and stale, like the butt of
    a dead cigar, —

The butt of a dead cigar you are bound to keep in
your pocket, —
With never a new one to light tho' it's charred and
black to the socket.

Open the old cigar-box, — let me consider a while, —
Here is a mild Manilla, — there is a wifely smile.

Which is the better portion, — bondage bought with a
ring,
Or a harem of dusky beauties, fifty tied in a string?

Counsellors cunning and silent — comforters true and
tried,
And never a one of the fifty to sneer at a rival bride.

Thought in the early morning, solace in time of woes,
Peace in the hush of the twilight, balm ere my eyelids
close.

This will the fifty give me, asking nought in return,
With only a *Suttee's* passion, — to do their duty and
burn.

This will the fifty give me.   When they are spent and
dead,
Five times other fifties shall be my servants instead.

The furrows of far-off Java, the isles of the Spanish
Main,
When they hear my harem is empty, will send me my
brides again.

I will take no heed to their raiment, nor food for their
    mouths withal,
So long as the gulls are nesting, so long as the
    showers fall.

I will scent 'em with best vanilla, with tea will I
    temper their hides,
And the Moor and the Mormon shall envy, who read
    of the tale of my brides.

For Maggie has written a letter to give me my choice
    between
The wee little whimpering Love and the great god
    Nick o' Teen.

And I have been servant of Love for barely a twelve-
    month clear.
But I have been Priest of Partagas a matter of seven
    year;

And the gloom of my bachelor days is flecked with
    the cheery light
Of stumps that I burned to Friendship and Pleasure
    and Work and Fight.

And I turn my eyes to the future that Maggie and I
    must prove,
But the only light on the marshes is the Will-o'-the-
    Wisp of Love.

Will it see me safe through my journey, or leave me
    bogged in the mire?
Since a puff of tobacco can cloud it, shall I follow
    the fitful fire?

Open the old cigar-box, — let me consider anew, —
Old friends, and who is Maggie that I should abandon
    you ?

A million surplus Maggies are willing to bear the
    yoke;
And a woman is only a woman, but a good cigar is a
    Smoke.

Light me another Cuba: I hold to my first-sworn
    vows,
If Maggie will have no rival, I 'll have no Maggie for
    spouse !

                        RUDYARD KIPLING.

ON A BROKEN PIPE.

NEGLECTED now it lies, a cold clay form,
    So late with living inspirations warm;
Type of all other creatures formed of clay —
What more than it for epitaph have they?

A VALENTINE.

WHAT'S my love's name? Guess her name.
    Nina? No.
    Alina? No.
It does end with "ina," though.
Guess again. Christina? No;
Guess again. Wilhelmina? No.
She reciprocates my flame,
Cheers me wheresoe'er I go,
Never forward, never coy,
She is evermore my joy.
Oh, the rapture! oh, the bliss!
When I met my darling's kiss.
Oh, I love her form to greet!
Oh, her breath is passing sweet!
Who could help but love her so?
Nicotina, mistress mine,
Thou shalt be my Valentine.

                                    ANON.

MY CIGARETTE.

MY cigarette! The amulet
    That charms afar unrest and sorrow,
The magic wand that, far beyond
    To-day, can conjure up to-morrow.

Like love's desire, thy crown of fire
  So softly with the twilight blending;
And ah, meseems a poet's dreams
  Are in thy wreaths of smoke ascending.

My cigarette! Can I forget
  How Kate and I, in sunny weather,
Sat in the shade the elm-tree made
  And rolled the fragrant weed together?
I at her side, beatified
  To hold and guide her fingers willing;
She rolling slow the papers snow,
  Putting my heart in with the filling.

My cigarette! I see her yet,
  The white smoke from her red lips curling,
Her dreaming eyes, her soft replies,
  Her gentle sighs, her laughter purling!
Ah, dainty roll, whose parting soul
  Ebbs out in many a snowy billow,
I too would burn, if I could earn
  Upon her lips so soft a pillow.

Ah, cigarette! The gay coquette
  Has long forgot the flame she lighted;
And you and I unthinking by
  Alike are thrown, alike are slighted.
The darkness gathers fast without,
  A raindrop on my window plashes;
My cigarette and heart are out,
  And naught is left me but the ashes.

                              CHESTER A. SNYDER.

THE PIPE CRITIC.

SAY, pipe, let 's talk of love;
    Canst aid me ?   By my life,
I 'll ask not gods above
    To help me choose a wife ;
But to thy gentle self I 'll give the puzzling strife.

Thy color let me find,
    And blue like smoke her eyes ;
A healthy store her mind
    As that which in thee lies, —
An evanescent draft, whose incense mounts the skies.

And, pipe, a breath like thine ;
    Her hair an amber gold,
And wrought in shapes as fine
    As that which now I hold ;
A grace in every limb, her form thy slender mould.

And when her lips I kiss,
    Oh, may she burn like thee,
And strive to give me bliss !
    A comforter to be
When friends wax cold, time fades, and all departs
       from me.

And may she hide in smoke,
    As you, my friend, have done,
The failings that would choke
    My virtues every one,
Turn grief to laughing jest, or painful thought to
        fun.

Her aid be such as thine
    To stir my brain a bit.
When 'round this hearth of mine
    Friends sit and banter wit,
She 'll shape a well-turned phrase, a subtle jest to
        hit.

In short, my sole delight
    (Why, pipe, you sputter so!),
Whose angel visage bright
    (And at me ashes throw!)
Shall never rival fear.   You 're jealous now, I know.

Nay, pipe, I 'll not leave thee;
    For of thy gifts there 's one
That 's passing dear to me
    Whose equal she 'd have none, —
The gift of peace serene; she 'd have, alas, a
        tongue!

                            WALTER LITTLEFIELD.

A SONG WITHOUT A NAME.

AIR: "*The Vicar of Bray.*"

'TWAS in Queen Bess's golden days
  That smoking came in fashion;
And from the court it quickly spread
  Throughout the English nation.
The courtiers first the lesson learnt,
  And burn'd the fragrant treasure;
And e'en the queen herself, 't is said,
  Would sometimes share the pleasure.
But this is true, I will maintain, —
  And I am far from joking, —
Of all the pleasures men have found
  There 's none to equal smoking.

Then learned men and lawyers wise
  And grave divines and doctors
Found smoking help'd to clear the brain,
  And puff'd away in flocks, sirs;
Then business men and humble clerks
  And laborer and peasant
By smoking care would drive away,
  And make this life more pleasant.
For this is true, I will maintain, —
  And I am far from joking, —
Of all the pleasures men have found
  There 's none to equal smoking.

And from these times we modern men
  Great glory do inherit,
And wealth and learning and the strength
  Which makes the English spirit.
We have no care, we fear no foe,
  We pass our lifetime gayly,
But little think how much we owe
  To great Sir Walter Raleigh.
For this is true, I will maintain, —
  And I am far from joking, —
Of all the pleasures men have found
  There's none to equal smoking.

                              W. LLOYD.

AD NICOTINA.

"A Constrained Hyperbole."

LET others sing the praise of wine;
    I'll tolerate no queen
But one fair nymph of spotless line,
  The gentle Nicotine.
Her breath's as sweet as any flower's,
  No matter where it blows,
And makes this dull old world of ours
  The color of the rose.

There's not a pang but she can soothe,
  Nor spell but she can break,
And e'en the hardest lot can smooth,
  And bid us courage take.

Fair Nicotine! thou dost atone
  For many an aching heart;
And I for one will gladly own
  The magic of thine art.

Ah, "friendly traitress," "loving foe,"
  Forgive this loving lay;
For I, thy worshipper, would show
  The sweetness of thy sway.
"Sublime tobacco!" may thy reign
  Ne'er for one moment cease;
For thou, Great Plant, art kin to brain,
  And synonym for peace.

E. H. S.

MEERSCHAUM.

COME to me, O my meerschaum,
  For the vile street organs play;
And the torture they're inflicting
Will vanish quite away.

I open my study window
And into the twilight peer,
And my anxious eyes are watching
For the man with my evening beer.

In one hand is the shining pewter,
All amber the ale doth glow;
In t'other are long "churchwardens,"
As spotless and pure as snow.

Ah! what would the world be to us
Tobaccoless? — Fearful bore!
We should dread the day after to-morrow
Worse than the day before.

As the elephant's trunk to the creature,
Is the pipe to the man, I trow;
Useful and meditative
As the cud to the peaceful cow.

So to the world is smoking;
Through that we feel, with bliss
That, whatever worlds come after,
A jolly old world is this.

Come to me, O my meerschaum,
And whisper to me here,
If you like me better than coffee,
Than grog, or the bitter beer.

Oh! what are our biggest winnings,
If peaceful content we miss?
Though fortune may give us an innings
She seldom conveys us bliss.

You're better than all the fortunes
That ever were made or broke;
For a penny will always fill
And buy me content with a smoke.

                                   WRONGFELLOW.

I LIKE cigars
　　Beneath the stars,
Upon the waters blue.
To laugh and float
While rocks the boat
Upon the waves, — Don't you?

To rest the oar
And float to shore, —
While soft the moonbeams shine, —
To laugh and joke,
And idly smoke;
I think is quite divine.

　　　　　ELLA WHEELER WILCOX.

"A FREE PUFF."

DO you remember when first we met?
　　I was turning twenty — well! I don't forget
　　　　How I walked along,
　　　　Humming a song
Across the fields and down the lane
By the country road, and back again
To the dear old farm — three miles or more —
And brought you home from the village store.

Summer was passing — don't you recall
The splendid harvest we had that Fall,
And how when the Autumn died, — sober and
    brown, —
We trudged down the turnpike, and on to the town?

  Sweet black brierwood pipe of mine!
  If you were human you'd be half divine,
For when I've looked beyond the smoke, into your
      burning bowl
          In times of need
          You've been, indeed,
The only comfort, sweetest solace, of my overflowing
    soul.
We've been together nearly thirty years, old fellow!
And now, you must admit, we're both a trifle mellow.
We have had our share of joys and a deal of sorrows,
And while we're only waiting for a few more to-
    morrows,
  Others will come, and others will go,
  And Time will gather what Youth will sow;
  But we together will go down the rough
  Road to the end, and to the end — puff.

ARTHUR IRVING GRAY.

MY MEERSCHAUM PIPE.

OLD meerschaum pipe, I 'll fondly wipe
　　Thy scarred and blackened form,
For thou to me wilt ever be —
　　Whate'er betides the storm —
A casket filled with memories
　　Of life 's Auroral morn.

Thou once wert fair like ivory rare;
　　Spotless as lily white;
Thy curving lines, like tendril'd vines,
　　Were pleasing to the sight,
And in thine ample bowl there lurked
　　A promise of delight.

Like incense flung from censer swung
　　Before some sculptured shrine,
To float along with prayer and song
　　To realms of bliss divine, —
Ascend thy fragrant wreaths of smoke
　　And with my thoughts entwine.

Old pipe, old friend, o'er thee doth bend
　　The rainbow hues of life,
While sorrows roll across my soul,
　　And peace is turned to strife,
And Faith drifts o'er a sea of doubt
　　With desolation rife.

Alas, that man or pipe e'er can
   Wax old or know decay;
Alas, that heart from heart must part,
   Or Love can lose its sway.
And death in life should cast its pall
   Athwart the troubled way.

Tho' love be cross'd, and friends are lost,
   And severed every tie;
Tho' hopes are dead and joys have fled,
   And darkened is the sky;
We yet can warm each other's hearts,
   Old meerschaum pipe and I.

                    JOHNSON M. MUNDY.

A WARNING.

HE.

I LOATHE all books.   I hate to see
   The world and men through others' eyes;
My own are good enough for me.
   These scribbling fellows I despise;
      They bore me.
I used to try to read a bit,
But, when I did, a sleepy fit
      Came o'er me.

Yet here I sit with pensive look,
   Filling my pipe with fragrant loads,
Gazing in rapture at a book! —
   A free translation of the Odes
      Of Horace.
'T is owned by sweet Elizabeth,
And breathes a subtle, fragrant breath
      Of orris.

I longed for something that was hers
   To cheer me when I 'm feeling low;
I saw this book of paltry verse,
   And asked to take it home — and so
      She lent it.
I love her deep and tenderly,
Yet dare not tell my love, lest she
      Resent it.

I 'll learn to quote a stanza here,
   A couplet there.   I 'm very sure
'T would aid my suit could I appear
   Au fait in books and literature.
      I 'll do it!
This jingle I can quickly learn;
Then, hid in roses, I 'll return
      Her poet!

SHE.

The hateful man !   'T would vex a saint !
  Around my pretty, cherished book,
The odor vile, the noisome taint
  Of horrid, stale tobacco-smoke
        Yet lingers !
The hateful man, my book to spoil !
Patrick, the tongs — lest I should soil
        My fingers !

This lovely rose, these lilies frail,
  These violets he has sent to me
The odor of his pipe exhale !
  Am I to blame that I should be
        Enraged ?
Tell Mr. Simpson every time
He calls upon me, Patrick, I'm
        Engaged !

                              ARTHUR LOVELL.

TO THE REV. MR. NEWTON.

SAYS the Pipe to the Snuff-box, " I can't understand
    What the ladies and gentlemen see in your face,
That you are in fashion all over the land,
  And I am so much fallen into disgrace.

"Do but see what a pretty contemplative air
  I give to the company, — pray do but note 'em, —
You would think that the wise men of Greece were all
      there,
  Or, at least, would suppose them the wise men of
      Gotham.

"My breath is as sweet as the breath of blown roses,
  While you are a nuisance where'er you appear;
There is nothing but snivelling and blowing of noses,
  Such a noise as turns any man's stomach to hear."

Then, lifting his lid in a delicate way,
  And opening his mouth with a smile quite engaging,
The Box in reply was heard plainly to say,
  "What a silly dispute is this we are waging!

"If you have a little of merit to claim,
  You may thank the sweet-smelling Virginian weed;
And I, if I seem to deserve any blame,
  The before-mentioned drug in apology plead.

"Thus neither the praise nor the blame is our own,
  No room for a sneer, much less a cachinnus;
We are vehicles, not of tobacco alone,
  But of anything else they may choose to put in us."

                      WM. COWPER.

A LOSS.

HOW hard a thing it is to part
   From those we love and cherish;
How deeply does it pain one's heart
   To know all things must perish!

And when a friend and comrade dear
   Is lost to us forever,
We feel how frail are all things here,
   Since e'en best friends must sever.

I, too, have lost a friend, who broke
   Its power when care was near me;
And troubles disappeared in smoke
   When he was by to cheer me.

But as friends fall when valued most,
   Like fruit that over-ripe is,
My loved companion I have lost, —
   That friend my meerschaum pipe is!

Judy (1873).

THE TRUE LEUCOTHOË.

LET others praise the god of wine,
　　Or Venus, love, and beauty's smile;
I choose a theme not less divine, —
　　The plant that grows in Cuba's Isle.

The old Greeks err'd who bound with bays
　　Apollo's brow; the verdant crown
He wore, when measuring their days,
　　Grew in the West, where he went down.

An idle tale they also told;
　　They said he gave them frankincense,
Borne by some tree he loved of old;
　　If so, he gave a mere pretence.

For the true offspring of his love —
　　Tobacco — grew far o'er the sea,
Where Leucothoë from above
　　Led him as honey leads the bee,

Till on that plant he paus'd to gaze
　　Some moments ere he held his way,
And cheer her with his warmest rays,
　　Heedless of time or length of day.

Then with a sigh his brows he wreath'd
  With leaves that care and toil beguile,
And bless'd, as their perfume he breath'd,
  The plant that grows in Cuba's Isle.

ANON.

THOSE ASHES.

UP to the frescoed ceiling
    The smoke of my cigarette
In a sinuous spray is reeling,
  Forming flower and minaret.

What delicious landscape floating
  On perfumed wings I see;
Pale swans I am idly noting,
  And queens robed in filagree.

I see such delicious faces
  As ne'er man saw before,
And my fancy fondly chases
  Sweet maids on a fairy shore.

Now to bits my air-castle crashes,
  And those pictures I see no more;
My grandmother yells: " Them ashes —
  Don't drop them on the floor!"

R. K. MUNKITTRICK.

WHAT I LIKE.

TO lie with half-closed eyes, as in a dream,
  Upon the grassy bank of some calm stream —
        And smoke.

To climb with daring feet some rugged rock,
And sit aloft where gulls and curlews flock —
        And smoke.

To wander lonely on the ocean's brink,
And of the good old times to muse and think —
        And smoke.

To hide me in some deep and woody glen,
Far from unhealthy haunts of sordid men —
        And smoke.

To linger in some fairy haunted vale,
While all about me falls the moonlight pale —
        And smoke.

                        H. L.

MY MEERSCHAUMS.

LONG pipes and short ones, straight and curved,
  High carved and plain, dark-hued and creamy,
Slim tubes for cigarettes reserved,
  And stout ones for Havanas dreamy.

This cricket, on an amber spear
   Impaled, recalls that golden weather
When love and I, too young to fear
   Heartburn, smoked cigarettes together.

And even now — too old to take
   The little papered shams for flavor —
I light it oft for her sweet sake
   Who gave it, with her girlish favor.

And here's the mighty student bowl
   Whose tutoring in and after college
Has led me nearer wisdom's goal
   Than all I learned of text-book knowledge.

" It taught me ? "   Ay, to hold my tongue,
   To keep a-light, and yet burn slowly,
To break ill spells around me flung
   As with the enchanted whiff of Moly.

This nargileh, whose hue betrays
   Perique from soft Louisiana,
In Egypt once beguiled the days
   Of Tewfik's dreamy-eyed Sultana.

Speaking of color, — do you know
   A maid with eyes as darkly splendid
As are the hues that, rich and slow,
   On this Hungarian bowl have blended?

Can artist paint the fiery glints
  Of this quaint finger here beside it,
With amber nail, — the lustrous tints,
  A thousand Partagas have dyed it?

" And this old silver patched affair? "
  Well, sir, that meerschaum has its reasons
For showing marks of time and wear;
  For in its smoke through fifty seasons

My grandsire blew his cares away!
  And then, when done with life's sojourning,
At seventy-five dropped dead one day,
  That pipe between his set teeth burning!

" Killed him? "   No doubt! it 's apt to kill
  In fifty year's incessant using —
Some twenty pipes a day.   And still,
  On that ripe, well-filled, lifetime musing,

I envy oft so bright a part, —
  To live as long as life's a treasure;
To die of — not an aching heart,
  But — half a century of pleasure!

Well, well! I 'm boring you, no doubt;
  How these old memories will undo one —
I see you 've let your weed go out;
  That 's wrong!   Here, light yourself a new one!

                        CHARLES F. LUMMIS.

ODE TO TOBACCO.

THOU, who when fears attack
　Bidst them avaunt, and Black
Care, at the horseman's back
　　　Perching, unseatest;
Sweet when the morn is gray;
Sweet when they 've cleared away
Lunch; and at close of day
　　　Possibly sweetest!

I have a liking old
For thee, though manifold
Stories, I know, are told
　　　Not to thy credit:
How one (or two at most)
Drops make a cat a ghost, —
Useless, except to roast —
　　　Doctors have said it;

How they who use fusees
All grow by slow degrees
Brainless as chimpanzees,
　　　Meagre as lizards,
Go mad, and beat their wives,
Plunge (after shocking lives)
Razors and carving-knives
　　　Into their gizzards.

Confound such knavish tricks!
Yet know I five or six
Smokers who freely mix
      Still with their neighbors, —
Jones, who, I 'm glad to say,
Asked leave of Mrs. J.,
Daily absorbs a clay
      After his labors.

Cats may have had their goose
Cooked by tobacco juice;
Still, why deny its use
      Thoughtfully taken?
We 're not as tabbies are;
Smith, take a fresh cigar!
Jones, the tobacco jar!
      Here 's to thee, Bacon!

        C. S. CALVERLY.

ON RECEIPT OF A RARE PIPE.

I LIFTED off the lid with anxious care,
  Removed the wrappages, stripe after stripe,
And when the hidden contents were laid bare,
  My first remark was: "Mercy, what a pipe!"

A pipe of symmetry that matched its size,
  Mounted with metal bright, — a sight to see;
With the rich amber hue that smokers prize,
  Attesting both its age and pedigree.

A pipe to make the royal Friedrich jealous,
  Or the great Teufelsdröckh with envy gripe!
A man should hold some rank above his fellows
  To justify his smoking such a pipe!

What country gave it birth?   What blest of cities
  Saw it first kindle at the glowing coal?
What happy artist murmured, "Nunc dimittis,"
  When he had fashioned this transcendent bowl?

Has it been hoarded in a monarch's treasures?
  Was it a gift of peace, or prize of war?
Did the great Khalif in his "House of Pleasures"
  Wager and lose it to the good Zaafar?

It may have soothed mild Spenser's melancholy,
  While musing o'er traditions of the past,
Or graced the lips of brave Sir Walter Raleigh,
  Ere sage King Jamie blew his "*Counterblast.*"

Did it, safe hidden in some secret cavern,
  Escape that monarch's pipoclastic ken?
Has Shakespeare smoked it at the Mermaid Tavern,
  Quaffing a cup of sack with rare old Ben?

Ay, Shakespeare might have watched his vast creations
   Loom through its smoke, — the spectre-haunted
      Thane,
The Sisters at their ghostly invocations,
   The jealous Moor, and melancholy Dane.

Round its orbed haze and through its mazy ringlets,
   Titania may have led her elfin rout,
Or Ariel fanned it with his gauzy winglets,
   Or Puck danced in the bowl to put it out.

Vain are all fancies, — questions bring no answer;
   The smokers vanish, but the pipe remains;
He were indeed a subtle necromancer,
   Could read their records in its cloudy stains.

Nor this alone.   Its destiny may doom it
   To outlive e'en its use and history;
Some ploughman of the future may exhume it
   From soil now deep beneath the Eastern sea.

And, treasured by some antiquarian Stultus,
   It may to gaping visitors be shown
Labelled: "The symbol of some ancient cultus
   Conjecturally Phallic, but unknown."

Why do I thus recall the ancient quarrel
   Twixt Man and Time, that marks all earthly things?
Why labor to re-word the hackneyed moral
   Ὡς φύλλων γενεή, as Homer sings?

For this: Some links we forge are never broken;
   Some feelings claim exemption from decay;
And Love, of which this pipe is but the token,
   Shall last, though pipes and smokers pass away.

                     W. H. B

MY LITTLE BROWN PIPE.

I HAVE a little comforter,
   I carry in my pocket:
It is not any woman's face
   Set in a golden locket;
It is not any kind of purse;
   It is not book or letter,
But yet at times I really think
   That it is something better.

Oh, my pipe, my little brown pipe!
   How oft, at morning early,
When vexed with thoughts of coming toil,
   And just a little surly,
I sit with thee till things get clear,
   And all my plans grow steady,
And I can face the strife of life
   With all my senses steady.

No matter if my temper stands
  At stormy, fair, or clearing,
My pipe has not for any mood
  A word of angry sneering.
I always find it just the same,
  In care, or joy, or sorrow,
And what it is to-day I know
  It's sure to be to-morrow.

It helps me through the stress of life;
  It balances my losses;
It adds a charm to all my joys,
  And lightens all my crosses.
For through the wreathing, misty veil
  Joy has a softer splendor,
And life grows sweetly possible,
  And love more truly tender.

Oh, I have many richer joys!
  I do not underrate them,
And every man knows what I mean,
  I do not need to state them.
But this I say, — I 'd rather miss
  A deal of what 's called pleasure,
Than lose my little comforter,
  My little smoky treasure.

                    AMELIA E. BARR.

FORSAKEN of all comforts but these two, —
   My fagot and my pipe — I sit to muse
  On all my crosses, and almost excuse
The heavens for dealing with me as they do.
When Hope steps in, and, with a smiling brow,
   Such cheerful expectations doth infuse
   As makes me think ere long I cannot choose
But be some grandee, whatsoe'er I 'm now.
   But having spent my pipe, I then perceive
   That hopes and dreams are cousins, — both deceive.
Then mark I this conclusion in my mind,
   It's all one thing, — both tend into one scope, —
   To live upon Tobacco and on Hope:
The one's but smoke, the other is but wind.

SIR ROBERT AYTON.

'T WAS OFF THE BLUE CANARIES.

'TWAS off the blue Canary isles,
   A glorious summer day,
I sat upon the quarter deck,
   And whiffed my cares away;
And as the volumed smoke arose,
   Like incense in the air,
I breathed a sigh to think, in sooth,
   It was my last cigar.

I leaned upon the quarter rail,
   And looked down in the sea;
E'en there the purple wreath of smoke,
   Was curling gracefully;
Oh! what had I at such a time
   To do with wasting care?
Alas! the trembling tear proclaimed
   It was my last cigar.

I watched the ashes as it came
   Fast drawing toward the end;
I watched it as a friend would watch
   Beside a dying friend;
But still the flame swept slowly on;
   It vanished into air;
I threw it from me, — spare the tale, —
   It was my last cigar.

I 've seen the land of all I love
   Fade in the distance dim;
I 've watched above the blighted heart,
   Where once proud hope hath been;
But I 've never known a sorrow
   That could with that compare,
When off the blue Canaries
   I smoked my last cigar.

JOSEPH WARREN FABENS.

LATAKIA.

I.

WHEN all the panes are hung with frost,
    Wild wizard-work of silver lace,
I draw my sofa on the rug,
Before the ancient chimney-place.
Upon the painted tiles are mosques
And minarets, and here and there
A blind muezzin lifts his hands,
And calls the faithful unto prayer.
Folded in idle, twilight dreams,
I hear the hemlock chirp and sing,
As if within its ruddy core
It held the happy heart of Spring.
Ferdousi never sang like that,
Nor Saadi grave, nor Hafiz gay;
I lounge, and blow white rings of smoke,
And watch them rise and float away.

II.

The curling wreaths like turbans seem
Of silent slaves that come and go, —
Or Viziers, packed with craft and crime,
Whom I behead from time to time,
With pipe-stem, at a single blow.

And now and then a lingering cloud
Takes gracious form at my desire,
And at my side my lady stands,
Unwinds her veil with snowy hands, —
A shadowy shape, a breath of fire!

O Love, if you were only here
Beside me in this mellow light,
Though all the bitter winds should blow,
And all the ways be choked with snow,
'T would be a true Arabian night!

T. B. ALDRICH.

MY AFTER-DINNER CLOUD.

SOME sombre evening, when I sit
  And feed in solitude at home,
Perchance an ultra-bilious fit
  Paints all the world an orange chrome.

When Fear and Care and grim Despair
  Flock round me in a ghostly crowd,
One charm dispels them all in air, —
  I blow my after-dinner cloud.

'T is melancholy to devour
  The gentle chop in loneliness.
I look on six — my prandial hour —
  With dread not easy to express.

And yet for every penance done,
  Due compensation seems allow'd.
My penance o'er, its price is won, —
  I blow my after-dinner cloud.

My clay is *not* a Henry Clay, —
  I like it better on the whole;
And when I fill it, I can say,
  I drown my sorrows in the bowl.

For most I love my lowly pipe
  When weary, sad, and leaden-brow'd;
At such a time behold me ripe
  To blow my after-dinner cloud.

As gracefully the smoke ascends
  In columns from the weed beneath,
My friendly wizard, Fancy, lends
  A vivid shape to every wreath.

Strange memories of life or death
  Up from the cradle to the shroud,
Come forth as, with enchanter's breath,
  I blow my after-dinner cloud.

What wonder if it stills my care
  To quit the present for the past,
And summon back the things that were,
  Which only thus in vapor last?

What wonder if I envy not
  The rich, the giddy, and the proud,
Contented in this quiet spot
  To blow my after-dinner cloud?

HENRY S. LEIGH.

THE HAPPY SMOKING-GROUND.

WHEN that last pipe is smoked at last
    And pouch and pipe put by,
And Smoked and Smoker both alike
    In dust and ashes lie,
What of the Smoker?   Whither passed?
    Ah, will he smoke no more?
And will there be no golden cloud
    Upon the golden shore?
Ah! who shall say we cry in vain
    To Fate upon his hill,
For, howsoe'er we ask and ask,
    He goes on smoking still.
But, surely, 't were a bitter thing
    If other men pursue
Their various earthly joys again
    Beyond that distant blue,
If the poor Smoker might not ply
    His peaceful passion too.

If Indian braves may still up there
    On merry scalpings go,
And buried Britons rise again
    With arrow and with bow,
May not the Smoker hope to take
    His "cutty" from below?
So let us trust; and when at length
    You lay me 'neath the yew,
Forget not, O my friends, I pray,
    Pipes and tobacco too!

RICHARD LE GALLIENNE.

SWEET SMOKING PIPE.

SWEET smoking pipe; bright glowing stove,
    Companion still of my retreat,
Thou dost my gloomy thoughts remove,
    And purge my brain with gentle heat.

Tobacco, charmer of my mind,
    When, like the meteor's transient gleam,
Thy substance gone to air I find,
    I think, alas, my life's the same!

What else but lighted dust am I?
    Then shew'st me what my fate will be;
And when thy sinking ashes die,
    I learn that I must end like thee.

ANON.

CIGARETTE RINGS.

HOW it blows! How it rains! I 'll not turn out
 to-night;
I 'm too sleepy to read and too lazy to write;
So I 'll watch the blue rings, as they eddy and twirl,
And in gossamer wreathings coquettishly curl.
In the stillness of night and the sparseness of chimes
There 's a fleetness in fancy, a frolic in rhymes;
There 's a world of romance that persistently clings
To the azurine curving of Cigarette Rings!

What a picture comes back from the passed-away
 times!
They are lounging once more 'neath the sweet-scented
 limes;
See how closely he watches the Queen of Coquettes,
As her white hands roll deftly those small cigarettes!
He believes in her smiles and puts faith in her sighs
While he 's dazzled by light from her fathomless eyes.
Ah, the dearest of voices delightfully sings
Through the wind intertwining of Cigarette Rings!

How sweet was her song in the bright summer-time,
When winds whispered low 'neath the tremulous lime!
How sweet, too, that bunch of forget-me-nots blue —
The love he thought lasting, the words he thought true!
Ah, the words of a woman concerning such things
Are weak and unstable as Cigarette Rings!
      J. ASHBY-STERRY.

SMOKING SPIRITUALIZED.

THE following old poem was long ascribed, on apparently sufficient grounds, to the Rev. Ralph Erskine, or, as he designated himself, " Ralph Erskine, V. D. M." The peasantry throughout the North of England always called it "Erskine Song;" and not only is his name given as the author in numerous chap-books, but in his own volume of " Gospel Sonnets," from an early copy of which this version is transcribed. The discovery, however, by Mr. Collier of the First Part in a MSS. temp. James I., with the initials "G. W." affixed to it, has disposed of Erskine's claim to the honor of the entire authorship. G. W. is supposed to be George Wither; but this is purely conjectural, and it is not at all improbable that G. W. really stands for W. G., as it was a common practice among anonymous writers to reverse their initials.

The history, then, of the poem seems to be this: that the First Part, as it is now printed, originally constituted the whole production, being complete in itself; that the Second Part was afterwards added by the Rev. Ralph Erskine, and that both parts came subsequently to be ascribed to him, as his was the only name published in connection with the song. See " Ballads of the Peasantry," Bell's edition. Variants of this song will be found on pages 86 and 150 of the present collection; the first is ascribed to George Wither, and the other is taken from the first volume of " Pills to purge Melancholy."

PART I.

THIS Indian weed, now withered quite,
　　Tho' green at noon, cut down at night,
　　　Shows thy decay,
　　　All flesh is hay:
Thus think, and smoke tobacco.

The pipe, so lily-like and weak,
Does thus thy mortal state bespeak;
        Thou art e'en such —
        Gone with a touch:
Thus think, and smoke tobacco.

And when the smoke ascends on high,
Then thou behold'st the vanity
        Of worldly stuff —
        Gone with a puff:
Thus think, and smoke tobacco.

And when the pipe grows foul within,
Think on thy soul defiled with sin;
        For then the fire
        It doth require:
Thus think, and smoke tobacco.

And seest the ashes cast away,
Then to thyself thou mayest say,
        That to the dust
        Return thou must:
Thus think, and smoke tobacco.

Part II.

WAS this small plant for thee cut down?
    So was the Plant of Great Renown,
        Which Mercy sends
        For nobler ends:
Thus think, and smoke tobacco.

Does juice medicinal proceed
From such a naughty foreign weed?
　　　Then what's the power
　　　Of Jesse's Flower?
Thus think, and smoke tobacco.

The promise, like the pipe, inlays,
And by the mouth of faith conveys
　　　What virtue flows
　　　From Sharon's Rose:
Thus think, and smoke tobacco.

In vain the unlighted pipe you blow;
Your pains in outward means are so,
　　　'Till heavenly fire
　　　Your heart inspire:
Thus think, and smoke tobacco.

The smoke, like burning incense, towers
So should a praying heart of yours,
　　　With ardent cries,
　　　Surmount the skies:
Thus think, and smoke tobacco.

TOBACCO IS AN INDIAN WEED.

TOBACCO'S but an Indian weed,
　　Grows green at morn, cut down at eve;
It shows decay; we are but clay;
Think of this when you smoke tobacco.

The pipe that is so lily white,
Wherein so many take delight,
Is broke with a touch, — man's life is such;
Think of this when you smoke tobacco.

The pipe that is so foul within
Shows how man's soul is stained with sin,
And then the fire it doth require;
Think of this when you smoke tobacco.

The ashes that are left behind
Do serve to put us all in mind
That unto dust return we must;
Think of this when you smoke tobacco.

The smoke that does so high ascend
Shews us man's life must have an end;
The vapor's gone, — man's life is done;
Think of this when you smoke tobacco.

From "*Pills to Purge Melancholy.*'

TOBACCO.

LET poets rhyme of what they will,
    Youth, Beauty, Love, or Glory, still
        My theme shall be Tobacco!
Hail, weed, eclipsing every flow'r,
Of thee I fain would make my bow'r,
When fortune frowns, or tempests low'r,
        Mild comforter of woe!

They say in truth an angel's foot
First brought to life thy precious root,
    The source of every pleasure!
Descending from the skies he press'd
With hallowed touch Earth's yielding breast;
Forth sprang the plant, and then was bless'd,
    As man's chief treasure!

Throughout the world who knows thee not?
Of palace and of lowly cot
    The universal guest, —
The friend of Gentile, Turk, and Jew,
To all a stay, to none untrue,
The balm that can our ills subdue,
    And soothe us into rest!

With thee the poor man can abide
Oppression, want, the scorn of pride,
    The curse of penury.
Companion of his lonely state,
He is no longer desolate,
And still can brave an adverse fate
    With honest worth and thee!

All honor to the patriot bold
Who brought, instead of promised gold,
    Thy leaf to Britain's shore.
It cost him life; but thou shalt raise
A cloud of fragrance to his praise,
And bards shall hail in deathless lays
    The valiant knight of yore.

Ay, Raleigh ! thou wilt live till Time
Shall ring his last oblivious chime,
 The fruitful theme of story ;
And man in ages hence shall tell
How greatness, virtue, wisdom, fell,
When England sounded out thy knell,
 And dimmed her ancient glory.

And thou, O plant ! shalt keep his name
Unwithered in the scroll of fame,
 And teach us to remember ;
He gave with thee content and peace,
Bestow'd on life a longer lease,
And bidding every trouble cease,
 Made summer of December.

THOMAS JONES.

THE CIGAR.

SOME sigh for this and that,
 My wishes don't go far ;
The world may wag at will,
 So I have my cigar.

Some fret themselves to death
 With Whig and Tory jar ;
I don't care which is in,
 So I have my cigar.

Sir John requests my vote,
  And so does Mr. Marr;
I don't care how it goes,
  So I have my cigar.

Some want a German row,
  Some wish a Russian war;
I care not.   I 'm at peace
  So I have my cigar.

I never see the " Post,"
  I seldom read the " Star;"
The " Globe " I scarcely heed,
  So I have my cigar.

Honors have come to men
  My juniors at the Bar;
No matter — I can wait,
  So I have my cigar.

Ambition frets me not;
  A cab or glory's car
Are just the same to me,
  So I have my cigar.

I worship no vain gods,
  But serve the household **Lar**;
I 'm sure to be at home,
  So I have my cigar.

I do not seek for fame,
    A general with a scar;
A private let me be,
    So I have my cigar.

To have my choice among
    The toys of life's bazaar,
The deuce may take them all
    So I have my cigar.

Some minds are often tost
    By tempests like a tar;
I always seem in port,
    So I have my cigar.

The ardent flame of love,
    My bosom cannot char,
I smoke but do not burn,
    So I have my cigar.

They tell me Nancy Low
    Has married Mr. R.;
The jilt! but I can live,
    So I have my cigar.

                THOMAS HOOD.

PIPE AND TOBACCO.

WHEN my pipe burns bright and clear,
 The gods I need not envy here;
And as the smoke fades in the wind,
Our fleeting life it brings to mind.

Noble weed! that comforts life,
And art with calmest pleasures rife;
Heaven grant thee sunshine and warm rain,
And to thy planter health and gain.

Through thee, friend of my solitude,
With hope and patience I 'm endued,
Deep sinks thy power within my heart,
And cares and sorrows all depart.

Then let non-smokers rail forever;
Shall their hard words true friends dissever?
Pleasure 's too rare to cast away
My pipe, for what the railers say!

When love grows cool, thy fire still warms me,
When friends are fled, thy presence charms me;
If thou art full, though purse be bare,
I smoke, and cast away all care!

German Folk Song.

THE LATEST CONVERT.

I 'VE been in love some scores of times,
　　With Amy, Nellie, Katie, Mary —
To name them all would stretch my rhymes
　　From here as far as Demerary.

But each has wed some other man, —
　　Girls always do, I find, in real life, —
And I am left alone to scan
　　The horizon of my own ideal life.

I still survive.　I was, I think,
　　Not born to run in double harness;
I did not shirk my food and drink
　　When Nellie married Harry Carnice.

But I am wedded to my pipe !
　　That faithful friend, nought can provoke it;
Should it grow cold, I gently wipe
　　Its mouth, then fill it, light, and smoke it.

But it is sweet to kiss; and I
　　Should love to kiss a wife and pet her —
She scolds?　Straight to my pipe I fly;
　　Her scowls through fragrant smoke look better.

There 's merry Maud — with her I 'd dare
    To brave the matrimonial ocean;
She would not pout or fret, but wear
    A constant smile of sweet devotion.

How know I that she will not change,
    My wishes at defiance set?   Oh!
(Pray this in smallest type arrange)
    She smokes — at times — a cigareto.

                            F. W. LITTLETON HAY.

CONFESSION OF A CIGAR SMOKER.

I OWE to smoking, more or less,
    Through life the whole of my success;
With my cigar I 'm sage and wise, —
Without, I 'm dull as cloudy skies.
When smoking, all my ideas soar,
When not, they sink upon the floor.
The greatest men have all been smokers,
And so were all the greatest jokers.
Then ye who 'd bid adieu to care,
Come here and smoke it into air.

                            ANON.

SIR WALTER RALEIGH! name of worth,
    How sweet for thee to know
King James, who never smoked on earth,
    Is smoking down below.

THE SMOKER'S CALENDAR.

WHEN January's cold appears,
    A glowing pipe my spirit cheers:
And still it glads the length'ning day
'Neath February's milder sway.
When March's keener winds succeed,
What charms me like the burning weed
When April mounts the solar car,
I join him, puffing a cigar;
And May, so beautiful and bright,
Still finds the pleasing weed a-light.
To balmy zephyrs it gives zest
When June in gayest livery's drest.
Through July, Flora's offspring smile,
But still Nicotia's can beguile;
And August, when its fruits are ripe,
Matures my pleasure in a pipe.
September finds me in the garden,
Communing with a long churchwarden.
Even in the wane of dull October
I smoke my pipe and sip my "robar."
November's soaking show'rs require
The smoking pipe and blazing fire.
The darkest day in drear December's —
That's lighted by their glowing embers.

ANON

AN OLD SWEETHEART OF MINE.

AS one who cons at evening o'er an album all
     alone,
And muses on the faces of the friends that he has
     known,
So I turn the leaves of Fancy, till in shadowy design
I find the smiling features of an old sweetheart of
     mine.

The lamplight seems to glimmer with a flicker of
     surprise,
As I turn it low, to rest me of the dazzle in my eyes,
And light my pipe in silence, save a sigh that seems
     to yoke
Its fate with my tobacco, and to vanish with the
     smoke.

'T is a fragrant retrospection, for the loving thoughts
     that start
Into being are like perfumes from the blossom of the
     heart;
And to dream the old dreams over is a luxury divine —
When my truant fancies wander with that old sweet-
     heart of mine.

Though I hear, beneath my study, like a fluttering of
  wings,
The voices of my children and the mother as she
  sings,
I feel no twinge of conscience to deny me any theme
When Care has cast her anchor in the harbor of a
  dream.

In fact, to speak in earnest, I believe it adds a
  charm
To spice the good a trifle with a little dust of harm;
For I find an extra flavor in Memory's mellow wine
That makes me drink the deeper to that old sweet-
  heart of mine.

A face of lily-beauty, with a form of airy grace,
Floats out of my tobacco as the genii from the vase;
And I thrill beneath the glances of a pair of azure
  eyes,
As glowing as the summer and as tender as the skies.

I can see the pink sunbonnet and the little checkered
  dress
She wore when first I kissed her, and she answered
  the caress
With the written declaration that, "as surely as the
  vine
Grew round the stump," she loved me, — that old
  sweetheart of mine!

And again I feel the pressure of her slender little
    hand,
As we used to talk together of the future we had
    planned:
When I should be a poet, and with nothing else to do
But write the tender verses that she set the music to;

When we should live together in a cozy little cot,
Hid in a nest of roses, with a fairy garden-spot,
Where the vines were ever fruited, and the weather
    ever fine,
And the birds were ever singing for that old sweet-
    heart of mine;

And I should be her lover forever and a day,
And she my faithful sweetheart till the golden hair
    was gray;
And we should be so happy that when either's lips
    were dumb
They would not smile in heaven till the other's kiss
    had come.

But ah! my dream is broken by a step upon the stair,
And the door is softly opened, and my wife is stand-
    ing there!
Yet with eagerness and rapture all my visions I resign
To greet the living presence of that old sweetheart of
    mine.

                JAMES WHITCOMB RILEY.

A PIPE OF TOBACCO.

L ET the learned talk of books,
  The glutton of cooks,
The lover of Celia's soft smack — O !
    No mortal can boast
    So noble a toast
As a pipe of accepted tobacco.

  Let the soldier for fame,
  And a general's name,
In battle get many a thwack — O !
    Let who will have most,
    Who will rule the rooste,
Give me but a pipe of tobacco.

  Tobacco gives wit
  To the dullest old cit,
And makes him of politics crack — O !
    The lawyers i' the hall
    Were not able to bawl,
Were it not for a whiff of tobacco.

  The man whose chief glory
  Is telling a story,
Had never arrived at the smack — O !
    Between ever heying,
    And as I was saying,
Did he not take a whiff of tobacco.

The doctor who places
Much skill in grimaces,
And feels your pulse running tic-tack — **O !**
Would you know his chief skill?
It is only to fill
And smoke a good pipe of tobacco.

The courtiers alone
To this weed are not prone;
Would you know what 't is makes them **so slack** — O ?
'T was because it inclined
To be honest the mind,
And therefore they banished tobacco.

HENRY FIELDING.

FRIEND of my youth, companion of my later days,
What needs my Muse to sing thy various praise?
In country or in town, cn land or sea,
The weed is still delightful company.
In joy or sorrow, grief or racking pain,
We fly to thee for solace once again.
Delicious plant, by all the world consumed,
'T is pity thou, like man, to ashes too art doom'd.

ANON.

TOBACCO, some say, is a potent narcotic,
That rules half the world in a way quite despotic;
So, to punish him well for his wicked and merry tricks,
We 'll burn him forthwith, as they used to do heretics.

TO MY CIGAR.

THE warmth of thy glow,
   Well-lighted cigar,
Makes happy thoughts flow,
   And drives sorrow afar.

The stronger the wind blows,
   The brighter thou burnest!
The dreariest of life's woes,
   Less gloomy thou turnest!

As I feel on my lip
   Thy unselfish kiss,
Like thy flame-colored tip,
   All is rosy-hued bliss.

No longer does sorrow
   Lay weight on my heart;
And all fears of the morrow,
   In joy-dreams depart.

Sweet cheerer of sadness!
   Life's own happy star!
I greet thee with gladness,
   My friendly cigar!

           FRIEDRICH MARC.

CIGARS AND BEER.

H<small>ERE</small>
    With my beer
I sit,
While golden moments flit.
    Alas !
    They pass
Unheeded by ;
And, as they fly,
    I,
    Being dry,
    Sit idly sipping here
    My beer.

Oh, finer far
Than fame or riches are
The graceful smoke-wreaths of this cigar !
    Why
    Should I
    Weep, wail, or sigh ?
    What if luck has passed me by ?
What if my hopes are dead,
My pleasures fled ?
    Have I not still
    My fill
Of right good cheer, —
Cigars and beer ?

Go, whining youth,
Forsooth!
    Go, weep and wail,
    Sigh and grow pale,
    Weave melancholy rhymes
    On the old times,
Whose joys like shadowy ghosts appear, —
But leave me to my beer!
    Gold is dross,
    Love is loss;
So, if I gulp my sorrows down,
Or see them drown
In foamy draughts of old nut-brown,
Then do I wear the crown
    Without a cross!

GEORGE ARNOLD.

EFFUSION BY A CIGAR SMOKER.

WARRIORS! who from the cannon's mouth
    blow fire,
    Your fame to raise,
    Upon its blaze,
Alas! ye do but light your funeral pyre!
    Tempting Fate's stroke;
Ye fall, and all your glory ends in smoke.
Safe in my chair from wounds and woe,
My fire and smoke from mine own mouth I blow.

Ye booksellers! who deal, like me, in puffs,
   The public smokes,
   You and your hoax,
And turns your empty vapor to rebuffs.
   Ye through the nose
Pay for each puff; when mine the same way flows,
It does not run me into debt;
And thus, the more I fume, the less I fret.

Authors! created to be puff'd to death,
   And fill the mouth
   Of some uncouth
Bookselling wight, who sucks your brains and breath,
   Your leaves thus far
(Without its fire) resemble my cigar;
But vapid, uninspired, and flat:
When, when, O Bards, will ye *compose* like *that?*

Since life and the anxieties that share
   Our hopes and trust,
   Are smoke and dust,
Give me the smoke and dust that banish care.
   The roll'd leaf bring,
Which from its ashes, Phœnix-like, can spring;
The fragrant leaf whose magic balm
Can, like Nepenthe, all our sufferings charm.

Oh, what supreme beatitude is this!
   What soft and sweet
   Sensations greet
My soul, and wrap it in Elysian bliss!

I soar above
Dull earth in these ambrosial clouds, like Jove,
And from my empyrean height
Look down upon the world with calm delight.

HORACE SMITH.

A POT, AND A PIPE OF TOBACCO.

SOME praise taking snuff;
   And 't is pleasant enough
To those who have got the right knack, O!
      But give me, my boys,
      Those exquisite joys,
A pot, and a pipe of tobacco.

      When fume follows fume
      To the top of the room,
In circles pursuing their track, O!
      How sweet to inhale
      The health-giving gale
Of a pipe of Virginia tobacco.

      Let soldiers so bold
      For fame or for gold
Their enemies cut, slash, and hack, O!
      We have fire and smoke,
      Though all but in joke,
In a peaceable pipe of tobacco.

Should a mistress, unkind,
Be inconstant in mind,
And on your affections look black, O !
Let her wherrit and tiff,
'T will blow off in a whiff,
If you take but a pipe of tobacco.

The miserly elf,
Who, in hoarding his pelf,
Keeps body and soul on the rack, O !
Would he bless and be blest,
He might open his chest
By taking a pipe of tobacco.

Politicians so wise,
All ears and all eyes
For news, till their addled pates crack, O !
After puzzling their brains,
Will not get for their pains
The worth of a pipe of tobacco

If your land in the claw
Of a limb of the law
You trust, or your health to a quack, O !
'T is fifty to one
They 're both as soon gone
As you 'd puff out a pipe of tobacco.

Life's short, 't is agreed;
　　So we 'll try from the weed,
Of man a brief emblem to tack, **O**!
　　When his spirit ascends,
　　　Die he must, — and he ends
In dust, like a pipe of tobacco.

From " The Universal Songster,
or Museum of Mirth."

IF I WERE KING.

IF I were king, my pipe should be premier.
　　The skies of time and chance are seldom clear,
　We would inform them all, with bland blue weather.
Delight alone would need to shed a tear,
　For dream and deed should war no more together.

Art should aspire, yet ugliness be dear;
　Beauty, the shaft, should speed with wit for feather;
And love, sweet love, should never fall to sere,
　　　　If I were king.

But politics should find no harbour near;
　The Philistine should fear to slip his tether;
Tobacco should be duty free, and beer;
　In fact, in room of this, the age of leather,
An age of gold all radiant should appear,
　　　　If I were king.

W. E. HENLEY.

THE PIPE YOU MAKE YOURSELF.

THERE'S clay pipes an' briar pipes an' meer-
    schaum pipes as well,
There's plain pipes an' fancy pipes — things jes made
    to sell;
But any pipe that kin be bought fer marbles, chalk,
    or pelf,
Ain't ekal to the flaver of th' pipe you make yourself.

Jest take a common corn cob an' whittle out the
    middle,
Then plug up one end of it as tight as any fiddle;
Fit a stem into th' side an' lay her on th' shelf,
An' when she 's dry you take her down, that pipe you
    made yourself.

Cram her full clar to th' brim with nachral leaf, you
    bet —
'T will smoke a trifle better for bein' somewhat wet —
Take your worms and fishin' pole, and a jug along for
    health,
An' you 'll get a taste o' heaven from that pipe you
    made yourself.

There's clay pipes an' briar pipes an' meerschaum
    pipes as well,
There's plain pipes an' fancy pipes — things jes made
    to sell;
But any pipe that kin be bought for marbles, chalk,
    or pelf,
Ain't ekal to th' flaver of the pipe you make yourself.

                HENRY E. BROWN.

CHIBOUQUE.

AT Yeni-Djami, after Rhamadan,
    The pacha in his palace lolls at ease;
Latakieh fumes his sensual palate please,
While round-limbed almées dance near his divan.

Slaves lure away *ennui* with flowers and fan;
    And as his gem-tipped chibouque glows, he sees,
    In dreamy trance, those marvellous mysteries
The prophet sings of in the Al-Korán!

Pale, dusk-eyed girls, with sequin-studded hair,
    Dart through the opal clouds like agile deer,
    With sensuous curves his fancy to provoke, —
Delicious houris, ravishing and fair,
    Who to his vague and drowsy mind appear
    Like fragrant phantoms arabesqued in smoke!

                FRANCIS S. SALTUS.

IN ROTTEN ROW.

IN Rotten Row a cigarette
   I sat and smoked, with no regret
  For all the tumult that had been.
  The distances were still and green,
And streaked with shadows cool and wet.

Two sweethearts on a bench were set,
Two birds among the boughs were met;
  So love and song were heard and seen
     In Rotten Row.

A horse or two there was to fret
The soundless sand; but work and debt,
  Fair flowers and falling leaves between,
  While clocks are chiming clear and keen,
A man may very well forget
     In Rotten Row.
         W. E. HENLEY.

THE DUET.

I WAS smoking a cigarette;
    Maud, my wife, and the tenor, McKey,
Were singing together a blithe duet,
And days it were better I should forget
  Came suddenly back to me, —
Days when life seemed a gay masque ball,
And to love and be loved was the sum of it all.

As they sang together, the whole scene fled,
  The room's rich hangings, the sweet home air,
  Stately Maud, with her proud blond head,
And I seemed to see in her place instead
  A wealth of blue-black hair,
And a face, ah! your face — yours, Lisette;
A face it were wiser I should forget.

We were back — well, no matter when or where;
  But you remember, I know, Lisette.
I saw you, dainty and debonair,
With the very same look that you used to wear
  In the days I should forget.
And your lips, as red as the vintage we quaffed,
Were pearl-edged bumpers of wine when you laughed.

Two small slippers with big rosettes
  Peeped out under your kilt-skirt there,
While we sat smoking our cigarettes
(Oh, I shall be dust when my heart forgets!)
  And singing that self-same air;
And between the verses, for interlude,
I kissed your throat and your shoulders nude.

You were so full of a subtle fire,
  You were so warm and so sweet, Lisette;
You were everything men admire;
And there were no fetters to make us tire,
  For you were — a pretty grisette.
But you loved as only such natures can,
With a love that makes heaven or hell for a man.

.   .   .   .

They have ceased singing that old duet,
   Stately Maud and the tenor, McKey.
" You are burning your coat with your cigarette,
And *qu'avez vous*, dearest, your lids are wet,"
   Maud says, as she leans o'er me.
And I smile, and lie to her, husband-wise,
" Oh, it is nothing but smoke in my eyes."

               ELLA WHEELER WILCOX.

MY CIGARETTE.

MA pauvre petite,
    My little sweet,
    Why do you cry?
Why this small tear,
So pure and clear,
    In each blue eye?

" My cigarette —
I 'm smoking yet?"
    (I 'll be discreet.)
I toss it, see,
Away from me
    Into the street.

You see I do
All things for you.
    Come, let us sup.
(But, oh, what joy
To be that boy
    Who picked it up.)

               TOM HALL.

A BACHELOR'S VIEWS.

A PIPE, a book,
    A cosy nook,
A fire, — at least its embers;
    A dog, a glass: —
    'T is thus we pass
Such hours as one remembers.

    Who 'd wish to wed?
    Poor Cupid 's dead
These thousand years, I wager.
    The modern maid
    Is but a jade,
Not worth the time to cage her.

    In silken gown
    To "take" the town
Her first and last ambition.
    What good is she
    To you or me
Who have but a "position"?

    So let us drink
    To her, — but think
Of him who has to keep her;
    And *sans* a wife
    Let 's spend our life
In bachelordom, — it 's cheaper.

TOM HALL.

PIPES AND BEER.

BEFORE I was famous I used to sit
  In a dull old under-ground room I knew,
And sip cheap beer, and be glad for it,
  With a wild Bohemian friend or two.

And oh, it was joy to loiter thus,
  At peace in the heart of the city's stir,
Entombed, while life hurried over us,
  In our lazy bacchanal sepulchre.

There was artist George, with the blond Greek head,
  And the startling creeds, and the loose cravat;
There was splenetic journalistic Fred,
  Of the sharp retort and the shabby hat;

There was dreamy Frank, of the lounging gait,
  Who lived on nothing a year, or less,
And always meant to be something great,
  But only meant, and smoked to excess;

And last myself, whom their funny sneers
  Annoyed no whit as they laughed and said,
I listened to all their grand ideas
  And wrote them out for my daily bread!

The Teuton beer-bibbers came and went,
  Night after night, and stared, good folk,
At our table, noisy with argument,
  And our chronic aureoles of smoke.

And oh, my life! but we all loved well
   The talk, — free, fearless, keen, profound, —
The rockets of wit that flashed and fell
   In that dull old tavern under-ground!

But there came a change in my days at last,
   And fortune forgot to starve and stint,
And the people chose to admire aghast
   The book I had eaten dirt to print.

And new friends gathered about me then,
   New voices summoned me there and here;
The world went down in my dingy den,
   And drew me forth from the pipes and beer.

I took the stamp of my altered lot,
   As the sands of the certain seasons ran,
And slowly, whether I would or not,
   I felt myself growing a gentleman.

But now and then I would break the thrall,
   I would yield to a pang of dumb regret,
And steal to join them, and find them all,
   With the amber wassail near them yet, —

Find, and join them, and try to seem
   A fourth for the old queer merry three,
With my fame as much of a yearning dream
   As my morrow's dinner was wont to be.

But the wit would lag, and the mirth would lack,
    And the god of jollity hear no call,
And the prosperous broadcloth on my back
    Hung over their spirits like a pall!

It was not that they failed, each one, to try
    Their warmth of welcome to speak and show;
I should just have risen and said good-bye,
    With a haughty look, had they served me so.

It was rather that each would seem, instead,
    With not one vestige of spleen or pride,
Across a chasm of change to spread
    His greeting hands to the further side.

And our gladdest words rang strange and cold,
    Like the echoes of other long-lost words;
And the nights were no more the nights of old
    Than spring would be spring without the birds!

So they waned and waned, these visits of mine,
    'Till I married the heiress, ending here.
For if caste approves the cigars and wine,
    She must frown perforce upon pipes and beer.

And now 't is years since I saw these men,
    Years since I knew them living yet.
And of this alone I am sure since then, —
    That none has gained what he toiled to get.

For I keep strict watch on the world of art,
  And George, with his wide, rich-dowered brain!
His fervent fancy, his ardent heart,
  Though he greatly toiled, has toiled in vain.

And Fred, for all he may sparkle bright
  In caustic column, in clever quip,
Of a truth must still be hiding his light
  Beneath the bushel of journalship.

And dreamy Frank must be dreaming still,
  Lounging through life, if yet alive,
Smoking his vast preposterous fill,
  Lounging, smoking, striving to strive.

And I, the fourth in that old queer throng,
  Fourth and least, as my soul avows, —
I alone have been counted strong,
  I alone have the laurelled brows!

Well, and what has it all been worth?
  May not my soul to my soul confess
That "succeeding," here upon earth,
  Does not alway assume success?

I would cast, and gladly, from this gray head
  Its crown, to regain one sweet lost year
With artist George, with splenetic Fred,
  With dreamy Frank, with the pipes and beer!
                EDGAR FAWCETT.

A BACHELOR'S INVOCATION.

WHEN all my plans have come to grief,
    And every bill is due,
And every faith that 's worth belief
    Has proved itself untrue;
And when, as now, I 've jilted been
    By every girl I 've met,
Ah! then I flee for peace to thee,
    My darling cigarette.

Hail, sorceress! whose cloudy spells
    About my senses driven,
Alone can loose their prison cells
    And waft my soul to heaven.
Above all earthly loves, I swear,
    I hold thee best — and yet,
Would I could see a match for thee,
    My darling cigarette.

With lips unstained to thee I bring
    A lover's gentle kiss,
And woo thee, see, with this fair ring,
    And this, and this, and this.
But ah, the rings no sooner cease
    (Inconstant, vain coquette!)
Than, like the rest, thou vanishest
    In smoke, my cigarette.

                      Pall Mall Gazette.